HOW TO DEVELOP YOUR CHILD'S INTELLIGENCE

More Successful Adulthood by Providing More Adequate Childhood

By G. N. Getman, O.D., D.O.S.

Copyright © 1993 Optometric Extension Program Foundation, Inc.
   Reprinted 1995

Printed in the United States of America

Published by the Optometric Extension Program
2912 South Daimler Street
Santa Ana, CA 92705-5811

Library of Congress Cataloging-in-Publication Data

Getman, Gerald N.
   How to develop your child's intelligence : more successful adulthood
by providing more adequate childhood / G.N. Getman.
        p.   cm.
   Includes bibliographical references.
   ISBN 0-979780-05-1
   1. Children--Intelligence levels. 2. Motor learning--Study and teaching (Preschool) 3. Perceptual-motor learning--Study and teaching (Preschool) 4. Readiness for school. I. Title.
   BF432.C48G47 1993
   155.4' 13--dc20   92-41293
                                                      CIP

TABLE OF CONTENTS

All Children Are Members of the Human Race; Kinds and Ranges of
Intelligence; The Child Learns to Know His World by Exploring His
World; A Child Must Learn All He Knows; Sight and Vision Are Not
the Same Ability; Vision Problems Can Be Learning Problems; "Vision
Is Intelligence"; Primary Seeing Skills Are Essential to Reading Skills;
Parents Must Provide Basic Learning Opportunities

The Developmental Processes of Childhood: General Movement Patterns; Special Movement Patterns; Eye Movement Patterns; Communication Patterns; Visual Patterns; Visual Integrations; The Concepts of
Our World Are Learned

The Door to Intelligence; Cause or Effect?; Age Alone Does Not Provide School Readiness; Reading Is More Than Seeing Words; More
Technology, Less Skill; Early Appraisals, Less Problems

(Procedures for the Development of Spatial Appreciation and Spatial Orientations; Flexibility and Posture)

(Procedures for the Development of Manipulative Skills)

(Procedures for the development of Visual Inspection Skills)

(Procedures for the Development of Communication Skills); Language Is a Visual Activity; Vision and Audition Are a Team; Children Need to Talk to Themselves; Start Reading to Your Infant

(Procedures for the Development of Interpretation Skills); Not
Every Puzzle is Educational; "My Name is Me"; Where are You
Now, Mr. Palmer?"; Mr. McGuffey Revisited; Is Your Child an Ob-
server or a Participant?; Reading--the Most Complex of All Human
Abilities

"The first teachers a child has are his parents."

**TO
C.E.G.
OUR CHILDREN, AND NOW
THEIR CHILDREN
*for their invaluable
contributions and demonstrations
and to*
JOE
*for new and valuable insights
to the developmental sequence.***

MORE THAN THIRTY-FIVE YEARS LATER

It is surprising, or perhaps just interesting, that most of the concepts and suggestions presented in this book now enjoy more validity than they did when first published. This book started out in the mid-1950s as mimeographed sheets for the parents of the children being cared for in an optometric office because of unexplained academic problems. These were the children whose parents and teachers described them as "smart in everything--except school." They usually demonstrated "20/20 vision" with no unusual refractive conditions such as nearsightedness, astigmatism or extreme farsightedness. However, there were consistent problems on any school task that demanded visual concentration and visual discriminations. This material was prepared to help these children achieve the visual skills the classroom was demanding, and when it was put into book form in 1957 it contained less than 50 pages, with a few line drawings to illustrate some of the recommendations. Several national publishers were interested in the unique approach to vision development presented in the expanded manuscript but would only consider publication if the title would be changed. They insisted that intelligence was "God-given," predetermined by inheritance, and unchangeable. Therefore, they said, the title was inappropriate and unacceptable. Change the title and publication would be considered.

There can be no argument about man's intellectual potential being God-given!! However, the Almighty Architect, in His wisdom, also gave man the capabilities for the expansion and enhancement of this given intelligence. The conviction that this uniquely human characteristic could be positively influenced by carefully guided experiences in the childhood years led to the private publication of the 3rd edition in 1962. Although this book was still intended for parents, educators found it helpful in their approach to lesson planning and curriculum design. It soon became a supplementary textbook, or recommended reference book, in numerous teachers' colleges both in the United States and abroad. The book was then translated into French and German, but the English edition was still

1

the most popular everywhere, and is still shipped abroad in quantities.

This edition is now more important than any previous edition ... not because the original book was full of errors or misconceptions, but because so much more is now known about human development and intellectual development. Even more important, much more is now known about visual development in the human, and this is now a critical factor in the human ability to meet and cope with the demands of an increasingly complex culture. Thirty- five years ago we were still in an *industrial* culture. In the mid-1960s we found ourselves in an *information* explosion. Today every child and adult is expected to have the tools to survive in an increasingly high-tech culture. Today's child, on entering kindergarten, is expected to have the visual skills with which there will be the complete mastery of all the printed pages in the books laid before him in the primary grades. Suddenly, the computer keyboard and the computer screen are demanding visual and tactual skills very few children have even begun to achieve. This is like putting a 5-year-old at a piano and suddenly insisting upon a rendition of a Brahms Lullaby. Technology, and all of its pressures for intellectual abilities, has outpaced the essential development the child should acquire in the preschool years. In spite of all the warnings and all of the commentaries, parents and teachers are expecting adult behavior from children who have not yet had the experiences and benefits of childhood. We may well be in a situation where there may be no opportunity to recover childhood, but there is still the opportunity to help every child and young adult achieve the visual, tactual and auditory skills important to the language development that is so critically necessary for success in the symbolic world every individual now faces. Thus, it becomes more imperative than ever before that there be very serious consideration of How to Develop your Child's Intelligence.

G. N. Getman, O.D., D.O.S.

WRITTEN FOR ALL CHILDREN

May their tomorrows be fuller and intellectually richer than were their yesterdays.

This material was first prepared, and has now been revised, to serve a very specific purpose. It is again directed to every adult having any responsibility for the intellectual development of children in our contemporary culture. It is sincerely hoped it will give these adults a greater realization of their responsibilities and opportunities in the guidance of these children.

This book has been analyzed, critiqued, and approved by authorities in several fields. Many of their suggestions have been included with their original recommendations as those appeared in the earlier editions. These contributions have been of inestimable value. The names of these valued contributors will be known to only a few of the readers of this book. These individuals must be named here for two reasons: their names must not be lost, and none of what is presented here would have been possible without the guidance and instruction from each of them. They are: Glenna Bullis, of the Original Yale Clinic of Child Development, Yale University, New Haven, Conn.; A. M. Skeffington, O.D., D.O.S., L.H.D., of the Optometric Extension Program Foundation, Santa Ana, Calif.; Samuel Renshaw, Ph.D., Department of Experimental Psychology, Ohio State University, Columbus, Oh.; Darrell Boyd Harmon, Ph.D., Consulting Educationist, Austin, Tex.; George Sweeney, formerly Director of the Hope School for Retarded Children, Sioux Falls, S. Dak.; Elizabeth Freidus, formerly Director of the Gateway School, New York, N.Y.; Sheldon Rapport, Ph.D., formerly President of the Pathway School for Brain-injured Children, Audubon, Penn.

Gratitude must also be expressed to literally dozens of my optometric colleagues who have validated the concepts expressed here through their clinical applications and explorations and ... special thanks to literally thousands of parents, teachers and children who have followed these recommendations through to greater successes in both academia and everyday life.

Back in 1962, the comment was made that some of this material might not completely agree with the "present educational methods."

It is a bit strange that this same comment can be made today, but the numerous positive responses from teachers encourages further suggestions even though there may still be some differences in approach. Every reader is urged to realize there has never been any intent to encroach upon education ... its methods or philosophies. All of the concepts presented here are based upon what is now known about human development and the human behavior now recognized as the learning process. There is not the slightest notion that this book contains panaceas for all of the problems children are having in meeting the academic demands being placed upon them. Neither is there the vaguest notion that all of the answers we need are contained in this book. This material is for everyone who wishes to gain a better understanding of the developmental processes so significant to the learning process. Hopefully the pursuit of ideas presented here may provide some of the clues we all need to help individual children cope more successfully with the extreme pressures of our culture. The use of these recommendations have shown them to be singularly effective in (a) developing learning readiness in preschool age children, (b) helping the primary school child apply what he has learned at school to everyday activities, and (c) assisting the child with special learning problems to achieve more adequate school and social performance. Thus, parents and clinicians may gain the insights to support and enhance the contributions of our educational system and its thousands of devoted classroom teachers. Hopefully, a "return to the basics" will be more than a repetition of the old three R's. Perhaps the "return to the basics" can be a thoughtful return to the programs that will allow children to develop those readiness abilities which will then permit the teacher to more effectively and successfully present the three R's to *every* child in *every* classroom.

This book is still primarily intended for parents. These individuals play the most important part in the young child's existence; they are the source of experiences which will shape the child's intelligence, and thus shape the entire future of the child. It is the parents' love and presence that will provide the environment in which every child can move toward the potentials a gracious God has designed into every newborn. This book is again written for all children in the sincere hope it will continue to be one of the most helpful handbooks continuing generations of parents have at hand.

HOW TO USE THIS BOOK

There are several ways in which this book can be used by parents to assist children toward greater personal achievement and performance.

1. You can make use of just those routines and suggestions checked for specific application in a child's particular situation.

   If this is your choice, only those pages containing the recommended routines need to be studied. This will give your child some help, but further skills can only be gained by the child's own practices. Some assistance is decidedly better than no help at all, but your child will receive only a small part of the guidance every child deserves.

2. You can make use of the routines checked as "take off" points and continue with variations and elaborations of the recommendations.

   If this is your chosen method of use, you will have to call upon your imagination and ingenuity to provide all the variety every child needs to avoid boredom and monotony. However, this is still short of providing the assistance every child can have.

3. You can make use of every routine and recommendation as the "take off" for guidance in every occasion and experience in everyday living. Thus, you can extend your child's abilities and skills toward their ultimate development.

   If this is your chosen method for the use of this book, it should be completely read and studied. Chapters I through II, and Chapter V can give you a whole concept of guidance for all children. As this concept is gained by you, every routine in Chapter IV can be made more effective and meaningful for your child.

Whichever of these three approaches you choose, we offer the following suggestions. *Quality* of practice is more important than *quantity* of practice, although the *amount* of practice must not be ignored. Your child may profit more from six five-minute sessions each day than he will from one 30-minute session--especially if the 30-minute session is fatiguing or frustrating. Learning to learn is like learning to play an instrument. It also requires a set daily routine which must be maintained. Learning always comes more effectively and permanently when the learner is interested, challenged and eager to achieve some goals. Variety and innovative applications of each procedure, practiced in short, frequent sessions will hold your child's interest and influence him to reach for greater skills in every activity. Just remember, please, extended *drill* on a procedure may increase the problem rather than modifying it toward more desirable results. Success *always* breeds success, and the training sessions then become activities at which your child will want to spend time in practice.

There must also be the recognition that too little practice will not bring the skills each child should have. There should be a routine set so there is *quality* practice at least five days a week. One cannot expect to become a concert pianist or a professional golfer with occasional practice sessions when there is nothing else to do. This concert, or professional, level of skill is exactly what every parent desires for his school child, and this expertise can only be acquired with a set and sensible discipline for routine practice.

The bright future which parents desire for their children must eventually come from the child's own abilities and skills. Learning cannot be done *for* a child, and no "smart pills" have yet been concocted. You must decide to what extent you will assist your child toward the brightest future by choosing the manner in which this book will be used.

> If I were asked what single qualification was necessary for one who has the care of children, I should say patience-- patience with their tempers, with their understandings, with their progress. It is not brilliant parts or great acquirements which are necessary for parents and teachers, but patience to go over first principles again and again, steadily to add a little every day, never to be irritated by willful or accidental hindrances.
>
> *Fenlon,*
> *From: The Dictionary of Thoughts*

PLEASE NOTE: *The pronouns, he, him and/or his, are being used throughout this book to refer to all children and parents, both male and female. These pronouns are used to permit the grammatical freedom which makes reading easier and more understandabie.*

LEARNING ACTIVITIES

INTRODUCTION

When G.N. Getman, O.D., D.O.S., Sc.D., died in 1990 he left a legacy on child development. A prolific author and lecturer, he shared his knowledge and ideas about children and their development thousands of times all over the world. He is recognized internationally by parents, educators, psychologists and behavioral optometrists.

This book has been reprinted many times and updated frequently. The information herein is timeless. It is difficult to imagine that these concepts regarding child development will ever be outdated. Dr. Getman's insight into how children learn has been substantiated in many research projects and numerous publications. His contributions have been recognized by many organizations that are involved with children and their learning abilities.

We all miss Gerry Getman!—We are pleased to announce that the proceeds from this book will be used for additional publications in the field of child development. For additional information please contact the publisher:

Optometric Extension Program Foundation
2912 South Daimler Street
Santa Ana, CA 92705-5811

G.N. Getman Memorial Fund Committee
Dr. Beth Ballinger
Dr. Greg Gilman
Dr. Robyn Rakov

CHAPTER I.
WHO IS YOUR CHILD'S
TEACHER?

The efforts of many experimenters and researchers in the fields which deal with human behavior begin to show a renewed interest in the young child. All this work points out the need for better understanding of the early foundations of human behavior. An adequate understanding of the adult is possible only when there is a full understanding of the childhood whence he came.[1,2,3,4]

(Reference numbers indicate a selected list of authors and texts for further study and are listed in order in back of book.)

This renewed interest has given investigators bi-directional information. First, it brings more knowledge of both child and adult. Second, and probably much more important, it has brought the knowledge of how to assure *more successful adulthood by providing a more adequate childhood.* It is interesting to note that in this day of materialism and cultural conveniences the need for the simple basics of living are vital to this adequate childhood of which we speak. It is rather alarming to consider that our cultural advances may have deprived more than they have benefited our children. The primary experiences with many common things--what they are for and how they work--are no longer available

Figure 1. The full understanding of childhood begins in those pre-bedtime moments of personal conversation between parent and infant. These few moments each day are the foundations of all parent-child communication and establish the rapport upon which intellectual development will thrive.

to children. A wall switch is a very poor teacher, with its hidden, complex electrical systems that have replaced the common experimental activities. The common things of life are the great things of life. These common things provide the experiences of childhood. These experiences can enhance the intellectual development so necessary to successful adulthood.[5,6,7,8,9,10,11,12]

ALL CHILDREN ARE MEMBERS OF THE HUMAN RACE

There is a new awareness of all children--the so-called normal, the exceptional, the slow learner, the handicapped. There is a tendency to categorize children who fit these classifications almost to the point of ignoring that *all* children are still members of the unique human race. These groupings label children as being different and there are very different methods of guidance and care for each group. This is unfortunate because it leads to confusion and ignores the basic and indisputable sequences of human development which have been established and validated in the field of study known as Child Development. Airplanes are airplanes, cars are cars, and TV sets are TV sets, regardless of size, shape or model, and each operates and performs on a basic principle which is unique but common to each. Somehow in dealing with children the fact that they are children and belong to the human race, which has its unique commonality, is frequently overlooked. If a child, for some environmental, genetic or traumatic reason, does not fit into the acceptable social patterns (which have been too greatly over-emphasized in our culture), then this child is labeled without enough consideration of his membership in the human race. Thus, more concern and emphasis is directed to his "defect" or "difference" than is given to his normality or belongingness within the total category that we call human beings.[13,14,15,16,17]

A child is a child, regardless of any category into which society may place him. His growth, development, behavior, performance and intellectual achievements will follow the natural laws which apply to all human beings.

Perhaps we should recognize that any child who survives must possess more of the normal than subnormal or abnormal or he would not have survived. If this is an acceptable assumption, we must look at what he *has* with much more diligence than we look at what he *has not*. Only in this manner and from this viewpoint can we obtain an effective, constructive and contributing philosophy of more adequate guidance toward a more adequate childhood. Only from this viewpoint can we set the stages for the intellectual development now known to be the result of the child's *own* activities and participations in *his* own world.[20,8,10]

KINDS AND RANGES OF INTELLIGENCE

Intelligence in the human is most interesting. The research of the past quarter century shows forcibly that intellect is not as rigid nor predetermined as was thought. Undoubtedly there are upper (and probably lower) limits to biological intellectual growth set by the factors of heredity. There is now an increasing recognition of a *cultural* intelligence which comes to children via their contact with the printed page; their observations of the behavior of playmates, parents and society in general; and especially through their own experiences of action and participation within an environment which is meaningful *to them*. There is now evidence that this cultural intelligence must be integrated with *biological* intelligence if a child is to become self-sufficient within our society.[21] If only one of these "intelligences" is present without the support and contributions of the other, the child cannot cope with the world and its present cultural and scientific demands. Thus, we can have children with adequate biological endowments who are the victims of the deprivations in basic experiences. Environmental circumstances, which do not provide the factors of cultural intellectual growth, cheat and defraud children more than we have realized. There is now much evidence that one plus one *can equal* three or four or even five when we consider the ranges of intelligence in the human race. One part of (a) biological intelligence, plus one part of (b) cultural intelligence, plus one part of (c) meaningful participation by the child, equals three or more units of total intelligence. The one part of meaningful participation by the child is the "yeast" which triples or quadruples the magnitude and importance of the ingredients. Tests of a child's IQ, which do not consider the factors of cultural intelligence and cultural participation, will often give a child a low and unfair scoring. Perhaps it is now valid to assume that ingredients (b) and (c) above are the "leavens" which bring about the frequently unexplained increases in IQ scores that

11

are seen when a child has full opportunity to learn under proper circumstances and guidance. If this is a valid assumption--and it seems such from the clinical and research evidence now pouring in--parents can and must provide the opportunities for the leavening.[22,8,23,24,25,14,26]

To give an example, a Dr. Spitz had an opportunity to study nearly 200 World War II orphans in two Swiss institutions. These children averaged 1 year of age. Approximately half of the children were given complete nursery and developmental guidance in an adequately staffed orphanage. The other half, in an understaffed institution, were properly cared for but received only the bare necessities of life. In addition, two control groups, consisting of children reared in the community outside the orphanage, were studied.

The children were tested and rated according to *a developmental quotient* (DQ) that used 100 as a base score. All children were again tested and rated four months later. The scores obtained by Dr. Spitz were:

		Beginning DQ	DQ 4 Mos. Later
Group 1.	Children in well-staffed nursery	101	105
Group 2.	Children in understaffed nursery	124	72
Group 3.	Village children from professional families	135	131
Group 4.	Village children from non-professional families	107	108

Group 1 gained one score unit in developmental quotient with each month of care and guidance. Group 2 lost 52 score units in four months of mere sustenance care. Group 3, who had the highest starting score, lost ground in the four months' time--perhaps because too many activities were done *for them*, and developmental experiences were missed by the child. Group 4 made a slight gain, which might be accounted for on the basis of other children in non-professional families. These children frequently seemed to benefit from the "lack of modern conveniences." Thirty percent of

Group 2 died in the first year of care. The remaining 70% of this group never regained the 124 DQ, nor even 100 DQ, with every effort to give them adequate care later.[27]

The significant point of this study is the effect of the deprivation of guidance and care. The child deteriorates to an alarming degree, may not even survive, and his loss of potential is very difficult to regain. One can therefore conclude that the very young child can be *irreparably damaged* when the opportunities for learning are not provided him.[7]

The most startling fact out of all study and research now shows (a) that most people spend their lifetimes in the lower ranges of their total intellectual possibilities, and (b) children in our civilization do not receive the fullest opportunities for the development of their cultural intelligence. Too many youngsters are "observers" of their world. Our society provides so many experiential shortcuts via movies, television, video games, etc. that children do not become involved in the many activities which could furnish the important opportunities to learn through participation.[10]

THE CHILD LEARNS TO KNOW HIS WORLD BY EXPLORING HIS WORLD

The first two or three years of a child's life may be termed the "Golden Years" of childhood, and should be full of participation

Figure 2. The pots and pans in the kitchen bring every learning process into action. No child should ever be deprived of such opportunities.

activity. It is this period of time when total body, hands, eyes, speech mechanism and ears begin to be the child's tools for learning. The movement of self through space, the manual and visual exploration and inspection of his world and its contents, vocalization of names, labels, needs and desires, are the full- time occupation of the small child. These activities start very early, and even the infant spends his wakeful moments visually inspecting and exploring his new surroundings.[18,28]

As the infant grows and progresses through time, all his faculties come into use so he may participate in his world.[3] His experiences are real and immediate, and thus he gains meanings, relationships and the reasons for things at his level. This lays important foundations for the understanding of the more complex world into which he will grow. Although he is born with the tissues of biological intelligence (brain), these only become useful to the child when he moves and acts, explores and manipulates, sees and describes, and makes use of the contents of his world. These are the foundations and building blocks for cultural intelligence.[8]

A CHILD MUST LEARN ALL HE KNOWS

Intelligence is a difficult thing to define, but it can be described as: the ability to make a judgment, decision, or action best suited to the problem of the moment, based upon the total knowledge gained from one's experiences. These experiences can be primary, or can be secondhand through the experiences of others. The latter, which

Figure 3. This picture of a cow was actually drawn by a first grader and was sent to the superintendent with a note from the school principal: "I am glad this class is scheduled for a visit to a farm the 20th of this month!"

are called vicarious experiences, are most available to us through the printed word. It is now evident that the printed word may not be adequate for a child without a meaningful background of primary experience. Here, also, children can merely be "observers" instead of "participants," and simply *reading* about the experiences of others does not necessarily add to the child's own background.[2] He should have primary experience in his background to which the story he reads can be related if there is to be any participation. The child who never leaves his square block in the city slums cannot possibly get the full intellectual impact of a story of a farm with its open spaces, trees, crops, animals and buildings. Give this same child one trip to the country, and what he reads becomes a whole new story because now it can be related to an experience that is meaningful to him. This example is gross--but real.

Parents do not fully realize how important little activities are to children. "Educational toys" are usually purchased because they appeal to the purchaser, who does not give enough thought to their use by the child. Conversations are often halted by busy parents, and the child's "Why?" is not fully answered. Children are instructed to "stay out of the way," and explorations and movements for experience are halted. There is a time and place for discipline, but it should not deprive a child of the opportunities by which his background of what, where, how, when and why is acquired. Formal education is the opportunity for extension and application

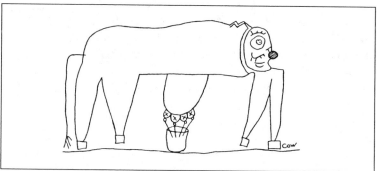

Figure 4. This picture was drawn by the same first grade child after the class took the field trip to visit the farm, where the little artist saw a real, live cow. However, just the day before the trip the class saw a film on clowns. Here is the second effort--a cow with a clown's face--but most of the fixtures are closer to being in their proper perspective.

of what a child knows. If the what, where, how, when and why period (the preschool years) is lacking, the formal school years suffer and cultural intelligence is stunted.

Parents must realize that *a child learns all he knows*. Very little comes with him at birth except the basic machinery for learning, and children must even *learn how to learn*. Infants do not arrive knowing how! The fact that an infant must learn to walk and talk is fully accepted by everyone. It is most important to know that the infant must also learn to see, hear, feel, smell, and taste--the machinery for each is present, but he must learn to use it.[29]

SIGHT AND VISION ARE NOT THE SAME ABILITY

A hundred years ago a man by the name of Snellen devised a sight testing procedure made of random letters of decreasing sizes. This test is the standard method of determining acuity of sight at a distance of 20 feet. Unfortunately, it has also become a criteria of visual ability in the minds of those who give no clinical thought to the purposes of vision. It is now necessary to define the differences between sight and vision if children are to have proper assistance in learning to see--or rather, in learning to understand what they see.

Sight is nothing more than a response to light. Sight is the reflex action of turning the eyes toward a light. This is called an "alerting response" and is observable in the newborn infant. Thus, the eyes are aligned with a light or brightness contrast, and to some degree come into focus upon it in the process of getting ready to see something.

Vision is the process of interpreting what is seen. Vision is the appropriate interpretative response to an effective light pattern. The response by the child that is appropriate is mainly a matter of his level of development and his previous experiences. Vision, then, is the process of getting meaning out of what is seen and is the skill of understanding and integrating what has been seen with the information that is also received through touch, hearing, and even taste and smell.[30]

Helen Keller, who is probably the most famous of all sightless persons, had highly developed visual skills. Her lack of sight deprived her of "eye" skills--so she developed visualization, visual imagination and perceptions by using the information given her by someone else through touch. Miss Keller is a splendid example of the fact that vision and visual skills involve more than eyes alone, and she certainly cannot be called a "blind" person.

It is important to realize that Miss Keller had a very normal childhood until the age of 3 or 4 when she then contracted a very serious illness, probably a meningitis. This normal early period allowed her to develop those basic skills upon which all of her substitute abilities could be built with the help of a tremendously insightful teacher.

Sight is the ability of the eye to transduce light rays into an (neural) energy that can be transmitted to the brain by the optical nervous system. Vision is what the brain does with the information that comes from the eyes. A sight test on the old- fashioned Snellen Chart is not a vision test. On the other hand, a complete vision test must include an appraisal of ocular acuity to be sure proper ocular information is being transmitted to the brain. Vision is an ability that is learned by a child and will be discussed more thoroughly in the next chapter of this book.[31]

There is another major criticism of the Snellen Test Chart which must be mentioned. Being a test for sight acuity at a distance of 20 feet, it gives absolutely no information regarding acuity of sight at the usual working distances of 14 to 20 inches. Parents are too frequently lulled into a sense of false security about their children's vision because a teacher, a school nurse, and even some uninformed "eye specialists" have given the children a rating of 20/20. Since the Snellen Test does not give any information about sight acuity, nor visual abilities *at study distances*, a child can still have a severe visual problem not identified by this very old and very inadequate test procedure. All parents should now insist on full information about their child's vision problems, even though he does not demonstrate a sight problem.[32]

VISION PROBLEMS CAN BE LEARNING PROBLEMS

Periodical literature is so full of misinformation, especially concerning vision, that a full understanding of the assistance which can be given children is lacking. Parents help their child to acquire walking and talking skills because they can observe the errors and mistakes of the child; the child's mistakes in vision and hearing are not so easily observed unless parents know what to look for. The mistakes or incompletions in *vision* are of vital importance because children will grow up to live in a world that demands more of vision than any other sense. They will not always be able to fall back on the other avenues of information (touch, hearing, taste and smell) to interpret everything that confronts them. They will frequently have to make their discriminations and judgments through their visual interpretations alone. In fact, nearly all their information will come to them through the visual mechanism. It has been said that 85% of an adult's daily intellectual decisions are based upon what is seen, or what has been seen in the past.[33,34]

It is also most important for parents to know that only a very small percentage of children are born with "eye defects." It is not conceivable that nature would allow a child to start life with an "eye defect" any more often than other defects occur. Studies at one of the largest children's hospitals in the United States shows that less than 2.4% of the infants had defective eyes (Chicago University Hospital, Chicago, Illinois).

A study of 160,000 children in Texas showed that 20% had vision problems at the age of 5, and 40% had vision problems by the age of 8. This indicated that so-called "eye defects"--nearsightedness, astigmatism, and excessive farsightedness--are related to the inadequacies of learning to use the visual mechanism in the first eight years of a child's life.[35] Many studies show that neither eyes nor the entire visual mechanism are physically and physiologically ready for the school reading load until 8 or 9 years of age. Yet, our children are now carrying a tremendously heavy load by 6 or 7 years of age. It may not be possible to speed up anatomical and functional maturity of the visual mechanism, but it is possible to ease, and possibly avoid, some of the stresses involved in the heavy nearpoint load by bolstering the skills and the abilities which the visual mechanism needs for achievement and efficient performance.

A behavioral optometrist, after a most comprehensive study of your child's *visual abilities*, will give you answers to when and why

Figure 5. Too many parents feel their children must learn to read by the middle of the first year in school. These pressures from parents may create more visual problems than will be outweighed by the fact that the child can recognize the words printed in his readers.

lenses will, or will not, assist your child. Glasses, which can be provided on a supportive and preventive basis by optometrists, are now assisting many thousands of children to rise above the "lower third" of their academic groups. Such glasses are not prescribed for a child as a result of his "wall chart acuities," but are prescribed for greater visual efficiency, and to counteract the stress created by too many books--too early.

In the near future every child will receive a complete preschool visual examination, just as he now receives a preschool dental and physical examination. Thus, parents will be fully informed and know how to give all necessary assistance to their child, who must meet and carry the school load and its demands upon vision.[36,37,38,39]

"VISION IS INTELLIGENCE"

A child may not always achieve the goals that our society has inconsiderately set for all children, but he need not forever remain at the lower levels of achievement because "he is a slow child." Or, if he is a "gifted" child, the goals and the uniformity of our social structure may be inadequate for him. In either case assistance that encourages better use of the child's capabilities can be provided by the understanding parent. This assistance will enhance and enlarge his intellectual possibilities for a more sufficient and purposeful adulthood within this visual world that lies before him. It is essential that parents know how to observe and rectify the mistakes in vision that occur, because a child's visual skills will largely determine the interpretation and comprehension of all things seen by him.

If you are wondering about this emphasis on vision, recall that children grow up to live in a visual world. Reputable authorities on human behavior now agree and state that vision and intelligence are very closely related. What a child *sees and understands* he can know; what a child knows determines his cultural intelligence.

PRIMARY SEEING SKILLS ARE ESSENTIAL TO READING SKILLS

The human being is superior to all other forms of life mainly because of his capacity to interpret the printed page. The ability to read is the highest level of intellectual performance and it is the goal held by all parents for their children. This is a severe goal to set for *all* children. The interpretation of the marks on the paper--which we call words--is not achieved by every child. In fact, some children should not be pressured toward the ability to read until much time and guidance have established all possible precepts and concepts in the everyday cultural experience areas.[7,40,41,42]

No one is in the position of authority at this time to state definitely that the slow learner cannot gain reading skills.[43] On the other hand, there is much evidence to support the presently held conclusion that *every* child can be benefited to some degree by the meaningful activities and experiences which develop the visual skills that can lead the child *toward* reading ability. This ability to read symbols is an end result of many years of self-development and practice in seeing. It is not just something a child does when a certain time and place in life are reached. Therefore, it is essential that all parents know as much as possible about the foundations of reading skills.[44,45,46,47,48,49]

PARENTS MUST PROVIDE BASIC LEARNING OPPORTUNITIES

There are a number of authorities in the fields of education, psychology, optometry and child development who have contributed greatly to the better understanding of the importance and significance of the first 10 years of a child's life. The efforts of these authorities and the results of their studies and observations now provide us with the methods and procedures by which the parents can furnish the developmental experiences all children need and should have. These methods and procedures have come out of a century of attention and consideration given to children. Research has now established how children grow and develop--how they mature physically, physiologically and psychologically--how they learn--and, most important of all, the sequence and cycles of all these factors, which are essential to the greater adequacy, self-sufficiency and intellectual development of every child.

Many of these contributions and the information which comes from those who have studied children have been available only to professional people who deal with the child away from home. Yet, the greatest single fact out of all study and research emphasizes that *the first teachers a child has are his parents.*

Herewith are the adaptations of the work in the fields concerned

Figure 6. The eye-hand skills essential to academic success do not arrive with the child at birth. These come only when opportunities are provided to assure their development. The child who lacks these eye-hand skills will certainly have difficulty in all classroom tasks.

with children and the tremendously important years of early childhood. The author and his colleagues have already seen the dynamic and fruitful results of these recommendations and can now urge their application and use by *every interested parent*. Thus, every child can grow and develop and become more ready for assistance the professional teacher will give him as he progresses through the years of formal education.

CHAPTER II
THE BASIC SEQUENCE OF
DEVELOPMENT

The literature on the development of children is extensive and historically significant. Much of the early material is as valid today as when written in the 1800s. The soundness of the original philosophies came from very astute observations of children. However, some of the original reasons and theories for the behavior and performance of the young child have been revised through the knowledge gained in recent years. The biggest change in our understanding concerns the basic sequence of growth and development in the first five years of life. [18,50,51,52,4,12]

THE DEVELOPMENTAL PROCESSES OF CHILDHOOD

Figure 7. Well chosen toys can be the seedbed from which intelligence may sprout. The signals that arise from explorations of the mouth, hands, and eyes bring the visual tactual interpretations of size, shape, texture, solidity, weight, and temperature. From these come the visual skills for the mastery of the environment and this mastery is the genesis of intelligence.

There are several main developmental processes which account for the totality we call a child. While these must not be considered as separate processes, they must be described for convenience in discussion of the parental guidance available to children. The sequence of these development stages from birth through childhood is a continuous ebb and flow discussed separately only for the better understanding of the total child.

These processes include six sequential and interrelated areas of development. A child should be given the opportunity to extend his ability in each of these areas. When parent and professional guidance incorporates the child's visual participation in each activity, vision becomes the link between the activity and comprehension. Whenever vision is the steersman for a child's actions, his visually directed movements provide him with a more comprehensive experience. The processes are listed in the following order because they chronologically develop in this order from infancy onward. The sequence of the processes and the inclusion of the visual components in each contribute also to the integration of all abilities. Thus, the child is most likely to acquire the ultimate levels of personal, social, and academic achievement.

A. The Development of GENERAL MOVEMENT PATTERNS for Action

This is a primary process and lays the foundation for all performance and for all learning. Movement *is* learning; learning *requires* movement. This is the process by which a child learns to use his head, body, arms, legs and feet to move about in exploring his world and assists him in learning to use his eyes as the steering mechanism to guide these movements. The child's bone frame is the basic supporting structure; his muscles are the anatomical parts for action of the structure; and the nervous system is the "electrical circuit" for the "start," "control" and "stop" of all movements. His steering eyes alert him to the goals and provide the direction of movement for action.[53,54]

B. The Development of SPECIAL MOVEMENT PATTERNS of Action

This process is a derivative and an extension of the previous process. Here the child learns to use his body parts in unison to control and manipulate the things in his world. These special movement patterns, which will govern each part or group of parts, have their purpose and will play a particular role in the productive action of the total child. However, each part or group must develop through use before it can make contribution to the whole. These must all be learned by the child, and the better he learns them the more coordinated and skillful he becomes. "Grace" and "poise" are words we use to describe the results of general and special movement patterns in all bone-muscle-nerve development.[55]

One of the earliest special movement patterns that is achieved in infancy is the combination of eyes and hands. This eye-hand relationship is extremely complex, and it takes a child many years to gain ultimate skills in this combination. It is, however, one of the very earliest integrations the child achieves, and it is a prime contributor to intellectual development. Clinical research now provides evidence that a child's ability to discriminate differences in sounds, tones, noises, etc., and his ability to produce more acceptable speech sounds, are all closely related to his ability to integrate the special movement patterns of the visual-tactual mechanisms. The better his discriminations are in any one combination of processes the better will be his discriminations in all other processes. As the child learns to combine and to integrate the movements of eyes with the movements of hands, he is setting the pattern for the integrations of all other combinations which are possible in all of the information systems of the body.[56]

C. The Development of EYE MOVEMENT PATTERNS to Reduce Actions

Experience and practice in this process assist the child in learning the eye movement skills that are necessary for the quick and efficient visual inspection of his world. Practice and experience in this process assist him in learning to use vision to obtain information about his world without the movements previously needed for exploration and manipulation. The reduction of action that occurs here, as vision replaces general and/or special movements, is economically important. Hands are now free to become tools. The hands are less and less involved in manipulations for information (such as size, shape, weight and texture) and can be used by the child to reproduce the information obtained through vision. Eye movement patterns become a guide for the hand movement patterns that will produce a scribble, a line, and eventually a word. Now he can begin to copy what he sees, and the skill and freedom of the eye movement patterns let him see more and more so he can *duplicate* more and more through hands.[25,30]

Some children have difficulty in acquiring freedom and skill of eye movements. Many children are too passive and do not engage in the activities that assist them to develop speed and flexibility of eye movements. Every child should have a thorough optometric examination to be sure these abilities are present *before* he starts to school. His reading, writing and arithmetic success will depend largely upon how well his eyes move across the pages of his readers and workbooks. Since these movement skills are learned, they can be improved through training and guidance by the considerate parent.[57,38,39]

Figure 8. The classroom workbook demands more eye movement skills than it does hand movement skills. The full control of eye movements is essential to visual inspections, visual discriminations and the visual

D. The Development of COMMUNICATION PATTERNS to Replace Action

These are the processes which assist the child in learning to use his visual and movement experiences for communication with others. Experience, practice and guidance here will assist him to establish a relationship between vision and language, which will permit the exchange of information through speech.

Children learn to talk by imitation of others. The actual learning involves a very complex control of the muscles of the lips, mouth, tongue and throat. There are movement patterns in speech, just as there are movement patterns required for any other activity.[58]

There is a significant relationship between the movement patterns for seeing and the movement patterns for talking. The child who demonstrates a lack of eye movement control and a lack of speech control will probably show many inadequacies in the special movement patterns discussed under B. Here also we have the evidence that restriction of movement in one area of performance can, and frequently does, act as a restriction on other areas of performance. Again and again, we are reminded that a child is a totality and all performance skills are related and dependent upon each other. There is increasing evidence that undeveloped eye movement abilities can act as a restriction upon language development.

Children are frequently seen who have not acquired a vocabulary that indicates a concept of directions of movement. The child lacking full freedom of eye movements will have more than the usual difficulties with such words as "up," "down," "right," "left," "near," "far," etc. It is very interesting to note that many clinicians who have devoted much study to children and their performances are reporting an acceleration of language development during and after training of eye movements.

Communication with others is an essential activity for children. Some communication is achieved by the imitation of the movements of others. Effective communication must come through speech, and this provides a child with the very important opportunities to check his visual experiences with others. A child also learns to talk by describing or naming what he sees. This is the only opportunity he has to verify his visual discriminations and in the very same process he learns to see more by talking about things. Vision and language are closely related abilities--they support and extend each other while they save time and energy by replacing action.

E. The Development of VISUALIZATION PATTERNS to Substitute for Action, Speech and Time

These are the processes that assist a child in learning the visual interpretations of the likenesses and differences in objects, numbers and words. As he gains the ability to make these discriminations, he can gain further knowledge about his world from the printed page. The recognition of a particular number or word demands that the child make a mental search through visualization of other symbols that may or may not resemble the one he is looking at. A child cannot complete this search successfully if he cannot visualize. Visualization is also a learned ability. It includes the memory of things, people or places previously learned and is sometimes called "visual memory."[33,34]

A child calls up a "visual image" in his mind and matches new words against the image of those he already knows. A process of selection and elimination allows him to inspect and interpret the new one. This process also includes a very strong factor of experience because the symbols that have the most meaning out of primary experience are the easiest to visualize.

Practice and application of these processes also assist the child to understand that symbols can produce visualizations of actual or similar events in which he has participated. The child who does not read well is frequently the child who cannot visualize. Even though a child may be very adept at "word calling" and can appear to read fluently, his comprehension of the material will depend to a very great extent on how adequately he can visualize himself as a participant in the story. A fluent "word caller" may be able to remember the story long enough to tell it to someone else with fair accuracy of details. Research into the methods by which a child learns to read now leads us to believe that this child views the story as if he were an "observer" instead of a "participant." As a result, he does not take from, and retain, all of the information included in the story. These are usually the "book smart" children, who can pass every examination upon the material but cannot recall the pertinent information to assist them in governing their decisions and performance outside of the classroom.

Visualization is an ability that ignores time and space. It permits a child to sail with Columbus or Magellan; or it allows him to reexperience a happy weekend in the country at grandmother's house. It permits him to "attend" the actual event that he is viewing on television even though there may be thousands of miles between. Of even greater importance, visualization skills provide a child with a path and a goal for future activities. Thus, he can anticipate and prepare for the appropriate actions in the time that lies ahead of him.

Visualization patterns are substitutes for action, speech and time; these patterns are obvious to the alert observer of children and are usually described by the child as a period of "jes' thinkin' 'bout what I'm gonna do."

F. The Development of VISUAL INTEGRATIONS

This is the ultimate process in the development of a *total* child. It is the ultimate stage in the development of his intellectual capabilities and is the end result of the sequential and interwoven relationships that come out of all the processes itemized above. These integrations furnish the ability to interchange body mechanisms for the interpretation, understanding and concepts of our world and its contents. The simplest examples of this ability are in the eye-hand interchange. Here we humans can feel an object, and when visual-tactual integrations have progressed as they should, we can describe the appearance of the object without looking at it.

The most complex example is the visual interpretation of symbols- -words, formuli, maps, etc.--into speech or action of hands. Visual integrations are the most significant of all our interpretative skills because vision as a distance receptor can help us to understand our world more completely than any other sensory mechanism.[18,59,49] Audition is also a distance receptor, but texture, size, shape, direction, color and distances are not "informations" available to us through hearing as they are through seeing. The touch, taste and smell mechanisms need much more specific contact before they can furnish the information upon which decisions and

29

interpretations can be made.

Vision, therefore, is the process by which a child interprets and responds to his world, the objects and the academic, cultural and social tasks within this world. There are many "perceptions" to which a child reacts, but if development and experience have followed the usual and expected course through the first 10 years, a child learns to use vision as the primary process to guide his own actions. What he sees, how he sees it, how he interprets what he sees, and the speed and skill of visual recognition will determine the majority of his responsive activities.

THE CONCEPTS OF OUR WORLD ARE LEARNED

It is very important to understand one aspect of this elaborate developmental sequence. Most perceptions of our world and its contents are all gained from self outward in infancy and childhood. Thus, vision (which should become the supreme skill for more complete and adequate concepts of our world of people, objects, words, pictures, direction, distance, size, shape, color and texture) develops out of the sensory motor mechanisms of actual contact. Samuel Renshaw (former Professor in Department of Psychology, Ohio State University) states: "Vision develops under the tutelage of the active touch."[25]

The child's ability to perceive the details of similarities and differences, relationships and individualities within his world provides him with his "working" concepts.

All of these concepts are a part of the capabilities of the human being, but they do not come about by happenstance. It is stated above that these concepts are learned. Anything learned implies action and movement. Experience is the best teacher *only when* the experience involves *movement use* of the neuro-muscular system (general movement patterns), practice and repetition for the combination of parts and body mechanisms (special movement patterns), and the resulting interpretation of all information thus received and integrated by all body mechanisms.

One must immediately recognize the complexities and interrelationships within this basic sequence of development. It is no longer necessary, however, to be overawed by it because it is now well enough understood that it can be utilized and applied in child care and guidance. Some of the very complex neurological functions of the central nervous system are still not fully known, but clinical evidence now provides learning methods which are valid and proven. At the present level of knowledge in the fields related to child guidance, the results and methods *that can be utilized* can now be presented for application by parents, teachers and clinicians. As more knowledge is gained, more opportunities can be provided for children, but it is no longer necessary to wait for the completely scientific explanations of the neurological, biochemical and physiological mysteries. These are of supreme significance to the researcher and clinician, but even when completely understood will provide only background understanding, which must be conveyed to parents in "how-to" language--as it is now being presented in the following pages.

CHAPTER III
READING ABILITY THE
GOAL OF DEVELOPMENT

THE DOOR TO INTELLIGENCE

The two previous chapters of this book have given a brief overview of the role of parents, the needs of every child and the sequence of development. These chapters have implied that there are many skills and abilities completely unique to the human being. Speech for communication, vision for interpretation of symbols, and cognitive abilities for abstract reasoning and predictions are some of these skills which only the human being possesses. [60,61,3,18,6,62,10,11,57,63]

CAUSE OR RESULT?

More and more consideration is now being given to the ranges of these abilities in the efforts to assist the retarded or slow- learning youngsters. Children who are failures in reading and who are labeled by parents and educators as "non-readers," "word- blind" or "dyslexic" are becoming outcasts in our society. It is easy to understand why so much emphasis and attention has been given to a child's low vocabulary, his inadequate reading level and his immature reasoning skills. Too frequently these have been overemphasized as the *causes* of difficulty. We must always realize that these problems are the *end result* of the child's lack of development in the basic sequences discussed in Chapter II.

Some writers blame reading inabilities on "lack of phonics training," others blame it on parents. Many writers are roaming far and wide in seeking answers to the reading problem. Usually their conclusions merely add up to the fact that these children are having trouble--with little or no consideration of the child's lack of basic development as the reason for the difficulties! As a result, such a child is given intensive remedial attention, which too frequently consists of just more word drill and word practice. This is much the same as asking the novice at the piano to learn his basics by drill, drill, drill on a Beethoven Sonata with none of the preliminaries of keyboard fingering, tempo, key or note-to-note relationships. It seems strange that the stages have been set for a developmental sequence of learning in everything else a child is expected to acquire as a skill, and then we still persist in our attempts to teach a child to read by immediately thrusting him into the manipulation of symbols in kindergarten. (This seems even more strange when a search of the literature shows that the extensive work of Montessori[40] in the late 1890s and the more recent work of Monroe[47] and many others who laid out sound, developmental methods have been lost in the shuffle of confusion and panaceas.)

AGE ALONE DOES NOT PROVIDE SCHOOL READINESS

It is now known that most children, age 6, have not adequately acquired the coordinations and neuro-muscular controls essential to advanced learning tasks. Eye movement skills, the physiological maturities of the visual mechanisms and the integrations of vision, hearing and speech necessary for ultimate success in the reading load are not yet available to most primary grade children. The free and easy "play as I wish" preschool years do not, *in and of themselves*, provide what the child needs for the cultural activity known as reading. Kindergarten, when available to a child, gives him some chance to organize and acquire a few of the above skills, but even this advanced activity program *assumes* that most of the basic developmental skills are present.

Because so many children *do* learn to read, the ability to do it when a child reaches school age is too frequently taken for granted. The years of study of children by child psychologists, educators and optometrists have brought much knowledge about the skills required when one looks at and reads the straight and curled lines called letters. When one stops to realize that the three little curlicues—DOG—do not have the slightest resemblance to a furry, long-eared, four-legged animal, one begins to recognize the difficulty a child may have in keeping letter combinations in mind. Learning to recognize and interpret the letter combinations in a single primer is a tremendous task for a child. The wonder is that any of them learn to do it!

Actually the process of learning to read starts very early in a child's life. The skill of seeing the difference between Mommy and Daddy is the same skill necessary to see and know the difference between the words "on and "in," "then" and "than," or many other similar letter combinations. There is a sequence in learning to make these judgments and discriminations which is common to words, places or people.

READING IS MORE THAN SEEING WORDS

It is now also known that what we see and the meaning we get when we see it is much more than what eyes look at.[64] When eyes and vision give us full meaning about a thing, or the word for this thing, we can feel it *as if* we touched it, hear it *as if* it were audible, and say it *as if* we used our voice. The complete process when developed to its highest skill allows seeing, feeling, speech and hearing all to work integratively. Thus, any cue to any one of the four will bring additional interpretations via the other three. Vision is the common "trigger" for the whole process because we humans advance through time to live, work and play in a world almost completely filled with words, pictures, maps, formuli, graphs and numbers--"cues" that are accessible to vision alone. These are the symbols of civilization which must be translated and interpreted through the visual mechanisms of those who succeed in our culture.

A child's reading ability then is the ability to recognize representations or symbols that *stand for* the things, places and people that make up the world in which he lives. Everyday experiences in the five years before school age are very necessary and important to reading ability. What education calls "reading readiness" is a meaningful total of all the experiences of a child's first five years, but all children do not have the same experiences in these important years. There are many experiences in conversation, everyday play and trips to the market that can be provided by alert parents if they just know how. In this manner children can be better prepared for school and educational demands. Reading readiness can thus be assured by parents--instead of the happenstance approach to school, which most children have had until now.

This chapter, as written to this point, is just as appropriate as it was in 1962. However, the intervening years have brought culture shocks to our children no one expected in 1960. First of all, the classroom has changed significantly and the curriculum is more heavily loaded with symbolic and abstract materials and procedures. Computers are an example of the technology that outpaces the development of the physiological and intellectual abilities needed for complete mastery of the computer. The computer scientist insists that exposure to the machine is all that is needed to gain mastery of the machine. Is it not strange that in the process of this mastery of all the machines our industrial revolution has made available there have been more injuries than benefits? In instance after instance the human has had to make concessions, adaptations and compensations to the machines and the human loses more than he gains. The losses include all the problems which can now be categorized under the broad term "pollution." These losses also include the creativeness and imagination that are the true signs of intellectual development. Of course, all the products of the current technologies are now facts of life and will continue to have greater and greater impact upon everyone. It is imperative we realize that children's developmental needs have not changed but their readinesses for the impact of the technologies are less and less as technologies progress more and more.[65,66,67,68]

MORE TECHNOLOGY, LESS SKILL

This technological and cultural impact influences all areas of the child's development where the basic discrimination and interpretation skills are so essentially important. The full impact of the demands and stresses falling upon the young child is most evident in the development of the visual, tactual and auditory abilities. Because too many children spend too many hours in front of a television set, there is the radical reduction of all the movement skills, with the greatest delay being observed in hand dexterities and in visual tactual integrations. The comprehensive evaluations of these abilities, so essential to success in today's culture, show that abilities in visual tactual integrations, visual inspection and discrimination abilities, and visualization skills are lagging behind all the other skills so critically essential to classroom success. The clinicians who are fully trained in child development and the expected visual development in children are finding too many visual problems which interfere with reading readiness. The visual system is not functionally ready for school tasks until somewhere between the ages of 8 to 10, but the classroom demands for computer and textbook are being introduced as early as ages 4 to 6. There is now no chance to change, or delay, the technological onslaught. There MUST be consideration given to greater preparation and protection of the children caught in this onslaught.

EARLY APPRAISALS, LESS PROBLEMS

Two emphatic recommendations must be made to every adult responsible for children's progress in the academic environment. Since the classroom has become so heavily loaded with visual requirements, a comprehensive evaluation of the child's visual development must be made by a qualified and informed clinician. This will usually be the behavioral optometrist who fully appraises visual abilities and visual reserves at all near distances as well as clarity on the wall chart. Such carefully conducted evaluations will determine whether or not there is a visual problem that might be hindering classroom performance. Research and clinical data now proves that judiciously prescribed glasses for all study activities can significantly reduce the impact and the stresses being faced by students in the expanded visual tasks of the classroom. The proper glasses effectively increase the student's ability to complete the heavy reading load now common even in kindergarten.

Further, the recommendations being made in this book now need more than casual consideration and use. Those routines which directly apply to the development of all the visual skills must be given attention, but similar emphasis should be given to all of the routines relevant to the development of skills in the auditory, tactual and movement abilities. Studies and clinical observations made on children of every conceivable intellectual capacity show that every achievement problem must be approached and guided through the basic sequences of development as discussed in Chapter II. Furthermore, skills which are being developed in the classroom should be applied to the gamut of activities outside the classroom. This is a major factor in the progress of every child and is one of the prime responsibilities of parents. A child must not be allowed to close the door on life as he walks into a classroom. Neither must he be allowed to close the door on intellectual development as he leaves the classroom.

CHAPTER IV
HOW TO ASSURE YOUR CHILD'S ACADEMIC SUCCESS

In preparing a program of guidance for children and the development of their potential skills, parents should give particular attention to five major areas of activity. Although many of the suggestions given here may be interpreted as preschool activities, the child already in school and having any degree of difficulty in achieving in the primary grades will also benefit by these activities because they will give the child who is achieving "satisfactorily" the chance to extend and apply the formal skills he acquires in the classroom to every extracurricular activity. We must always realize that every child needs opportunities to extend and use the intellectual abilities he possesses; these are so frequently untapped!

The five areas of developmental activities to be discussed in the following pages are: A. General movement patterns for the development of exploratory skills, B. Special movement patterns for the development of manipulative skills, C. Eye movement patterns for the development of visual inspection and discrimination skills, D. Vision-language patterns for the development of communication skills, E. Visualization patterns for the development of cognitive skills. The last of these five will include the extension of visual integrations into the skill of concept formation.

These five areas are closely interrelated and have labels for descriptive purposes only. The total development of a child is the result of an interweaving of all these areas and, as previously stated, activity in any one area affects and brings responses in all other areas through integrative development. While this is undoubtedly true, the methods and routines given here are arranged to originate activity for the child so the learning emphasis falls into one of the above areas. Each of the routines selected for inclusion here has been carefully chosen because of its contribution to the readiness that assures a child of a greater success in the classroom.

Humans are constantly reaching new levels of readiness throughout their lifetime. This is spectacularly true of children whose readinesses for a new learning level are often very visible. A child may demonstrate his lack of a particular concept by his erratic, evasive or guess-type answers. The next moment, or perhaps the next day, his cognitive organizations bring forth a vivid demonstration of his acquisition of the concept. Cartoonists illustrate this event by putting a lighted bulb in the balloon over their character. It is as if a light does turn on, and it is frequently seen in the alert face and sparkling eyes of a child. Each "lighted bulb" denotes another level of readiness for new learning opportunities.

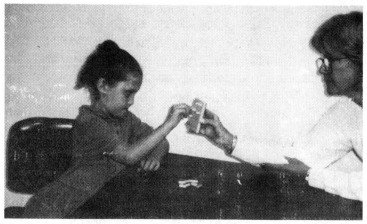

Figure 9. Getting and using a concept is a thrilling moment for a child. The joy of this moment is very real and the child's face will sparkle with the expression of: "Oh, now I know."

The sequence of A through E is based upon both the presently recognized sequences of development (Chapter II) and the sequences of maturation typical of the human child. The routines that follow are also given in the developmental order that is characteristic of children. The old law, "One must learn to creep before one can walk," is applied here so the more advanced skills can evolve properly and adequately from basic skills. This is the contribution of the field of child development and now provides an understanding of what is known as the "spiral of development,"(Arnold Gesell, "Child from 5 to 10": 58-9; "The embryology of behavior": 163-4.) which permits and assists the child to learn first things first toward the achievement of his ultimate potentials.[2,18,51,29,69,70]

A—GENERAL MOVEMENT PATTERNS

(Procedures for the development of spatial appreciation and spatial orientation skills)

Foundational to every intellectual activity of the human are the skills of directed movements and total motor coordination. The efficiency of muscle use is a prerequisite for the acquisition of all knowledge of the world surrounding us. Intelligent performance in our environment demands the mind be free to think about the world instead of being constrained by attention upon movements. It has been said: "Thoughts that never fully possess the muscles never fully possess the mind." This wise individual undoubtedly realized that the skill of mentally planning an action has to come out of the practice in the action itself so the muscles operate automatically-- "possessed by thought" that is appropriate to the action. To paraphrase an academic cliche: "The infant learns to move so he can then move to learn." It can be well summarized--all learning demands movement in some order at some level of consciousness. Unfortunately, all movement does not guarantee learning, and the most productive movement patterns need careful review.

The expectant mother is frequently aware that her unborn baby is already thrusting, kicking, stretching and turning. This is the early activity in which this baby is finding out what movement is and how to activate the muscles which are developing. There is probably no conscious effort as we generally think of it (although some researchers insist it is already a level of consciousness) but it is an established fact that this is the time in pregnancy when the actions of the infant are bringing the first proliferations and integrations of the nervous system and the movement system. There can be no doubt about the unique design of the movement system in the human, and its purposes are being appreciated more and more as there is a growing understanding of all the developmental processes essential to both physical and intellectual growth. If there is to be achievement of the ultimate potentials every child brings, there must be a greater recognition of why movement skills are so important.

Two primary aspects of all human movements can be identified. First, there is the acquisition of the skills of *mobility*. This is the process through which the infant progresses to find out how to move, what part to move, where to move, why to move, and *when* to move. All these organizations of general movement become significant to moving in response to the many stimuli that impinge upon an infant. Of these five variables, the emerging knowledge of *when* to move, and *when not* to move, becomes very significant because the skill of *immobility* is also a basic survival function. The skill of *not moving* is difficult to achieve because the human is designed to respond to stimuli and to react as quickly as possible. There are many children improperly diagnosed as "hyperactive" or "hyperkinetic" who have only NOT learned how NOT to move. In more common terms, these individuals have not learned the skills of relaxation-- how to turn off their muscles. The careful clinical observations of literally hundreds of children so diagnosed bring the emphatic evidence that drugs for hyperactivity also drug the cognitive processes, and very often these drugs are neither a reasonable nor productive tradeoff. Undoubtedly, there are some individuals whose neurological problems demand the carefully selected prescriptions of cautious clinicians but there is no scientific proof that such drugs are the only viable approach to all these children so labeled. Neither is there the slightest indication these drugs will, by some unexplained magic, automatically provide the child with those movement skills he has not yet achieved. The results of guidance and instruction by informed adaptive physical education teachers, movement specialists, physiotherapists, and a comparatively few occupational therapists, are bringing better answers on how to eliminate the *cause* of the hyperactivity rather than relying upon the random drugging of the *symptom*. The routines which follow provide excellent approaches to the skills of both *mobility* and *immobility* for all children, especially many of those who have been misdiagnosed and mislabeled "hyperactive."

There is now general agreement that "fine motor control can only emerge out of gross motor control." This book refers to "gross motor" activities as general movement patterns. It is also now widely agreed that all movement skills come from a very sequential development out of visually directed movement practice at all levels of both general and special motor actions. Is a ballet dancer demonstrating "gross motor" action *or* "fine motor" action? Is the professional football quarterback demonstrating "gross motor" action *or* "fine motor" action? Both the dancer and the quarterback are excellent examples of directed movement-- movement that is directed, monitored and modified by the visual system. To clarify some of the confusions which exist, this book will discuss *general* movements as those used by an individual to transport himself to a selected goal, and *special* movements are those used by the individual to inspect and manipulate the environment and its contents after arriving at a chosen goal.[53]

Undoubtedly, if general motor controls are lacking or inadequate for pathological reasons, the more specialized movements will be restricted or inefficient. When such a condition exists, an individual will demonstrate difficulties in coloring, cutting and pasting in kindergarten, and in writing in all of the following grades. Likewise, careful observations of these same individuals will expose difficulties in visual inspections, and the ability to visually scan lines of printed words. This individual will skip words or lines, and too frequently lose his place on the pages because these particular classroom activities are the ultimate in visually directed movements. Further, such a problem can be observed in the speech skills where the special motor abilities are so important to full language development. It is now time to consider all movement abilities as sequential and preliminary components of the total development of the individual. It is also important to understand this sequence of development in proper context and not as something that will automatically happen in a recess program designed only to wear off children's pent up energies.

Specific inadequacies in movement abilities can, in some instances, be the direct result of the stress imposed by the academic demands upon a child. These can too often be observed in the postural warps imposed upon children by desks too high or too low for the individual. Children do not all come in the same size, but the contemporary classroom is filled with desks that are all the same size. Explicit research shows these postural stresses are contributors to biochemical, dental, visual, and back problems that need not occur. The informed behavioral optometrist, whose comprehensive examination will evaluate the basic motor skills of the visual mechanism, will tell parents of such inadequacies should they exist in the child being examined. When such problems in the visual abilities are found, this optometrist will recommend carefully selected office therapies and home practice procedures to mediate the problems. These programs are called vision training and are most effective when provided under the supervision and direction of the optometrist. A technician, or therapist, may do the actual work of representing the routines to the patient, but for the protection of the individual the procedures must be judiciously determined by the optometrist and will follow prescriptions appropriate to each individual's needs.

Emphasis should be given here to creeping and its place in the sequence of development in all movement abilities. There is real significance in creeping for the exploration and emergence of total coordination. The omission of the creeping experiences, preliminary to walking practice, is clinically evident throughout childhood. For example, many retarded children rarely do any all- fours creeping (on hands and knees, or on hands and feet) in late infancy and this omission is almost always evident to the alert clinician who recognizes the lack of total coordination. A point of clarification MUST be made here and now!! It is completely invalid to assume that if a child did omit the usual creeping stage he should be without coordination in all movement patterns. Neither dare we assume a return to creeping, as a clinical procedure at later ages, will "cure" all the problems some individuals have in school. It is most desirable every child find and explore all of the creeping movements for the fullest possible familiarity with the movements available to him. References to creeping here are to call attention to the developmental sequence which is significant to the total progress toward that level of movement skill that will then free the mind for learning *after* learning to move.[7,14]

BASIC MOVEMENTS

It becomes more and more obvious that the primary purpose of the visual system is to serve as the guide for all of our movements safely and effectively through our surroundings. Before this guidance system can become the subconscious skill that it does in most individuals most individuals, there are some of the primitive and basic movements which most children need to review. Probably the most inherent of these is the position assumed by infants in relaxed wakefulness. This is known as the TNR (the tonic-neck-reflex). This is the posture in which the infant turns head to the side on which the arm is outstretched, with the leg on the same side extended. On the opposite side, the arm and the leg are both flexed. As both the right and the left TNRs are explored, the infant finds he has two sides and there is also the inherent opportunity to explore the first integrations of body parts. It also appears this is the time at which the infant finds the first eye-hand combinations and the first opportunity to visually observe and inspect his own movements. It is not unusual to find that those children who demonstrate learning problems did not fully experience these TNR movement patterns.[18]

Very few primary grade children will appreciate any request they return to infantile activities, even for a few moments of motor organization. The following procedure usually catches their cooperation. At the same time it permits concentration upon selected movements of the extremities and the review of the TNR without the need to maintain a gravitationally impossible erect posture.

a. Angels in the Snow, or Swimming on the Beach

Have your child lie on his back on the floor with legs straight and

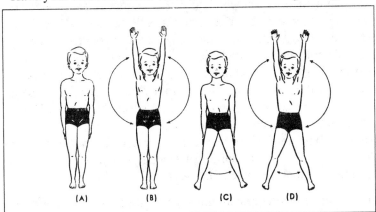

(A)   (B)   (C)   (D)

Figure 10. Angels in the Snow lets the child explore the movements of his extremities without having to maintain gravitational balance of the upright position.

arms at the sides (Position A, Figure 10). Both arms are then slid along the floor in a full arc to a position above the head (Position B, Figure 10). Instruct your child to "look up" at the hands when these reach the "up" position, and to look downward when arms are being returned to the sides of the body. Ask your child to repeat these arm movements until both move in unison, hands touching each other at the peak of the arc, and eyes are pointed at the hands as they touch. Next, arms are held at the sides while legs are moved apart as widely as possible, then moved back to the heels together position. Again, have your child look upward as legs move outward, and then look downward as heels come together. These movements should be practiced until there is observable fluidity and coordination of the movements of arms and legs (Position C, Figure 10).

As soon as these fluidities are noted, have your child move arms in the upward arc while moving legs apart (Position D, Figure 20). These upward and downward movements of the arms in coordination with the outward and inward movements of the legs should be practiced until there is fluid and coordinated movements of all four extremities. Since matching eye movements are impossible here, ask your child to *pretend* he is looking into a mirror where all the actions of arms and legs can be "seen." This can be one of the first experiences in visualization which will be discussed in extended detail later.

When all of the combined movements are smoothly executed, ask your child to begin moving only one extremity at a time. For example, move only the right arm through the upward arc. Now, ask your child to actually watch the hand in movement and to verbalize the action. "My right arm is down at my right side and now moving outward and upward to a position over my head. Now, my right arm is moving downward to my right side." If this is too complex a verbalization, request the most suitable words: "Right arm ... out ... up ... down to right side." This is practice in the eye-hand combination that can be a review of the TNR, and there is also the practice here in the labels of sidedness that will eventually become the labels of directionality.

Continue to incorporate all the visual and verbal actions with all the variations you can think of for Angels in the Snow. These will become more difficult as the more complex combinations and varieties of movement are explored, but the integrations of learning systems here can have significant impact upon the more advanced activities in which greater skill of coordination is demanded. It is essential there be every possible exploration of every possible movement of the extremities in isolation, combination and alternation. Have your child explore and "invent" ways to move arms, head, eyes and legs while finding new ways of telling you what is being done. These procedures, done in this fashion, will be possible for nearly every child, and even the spastic or palsied child can gain greater body flexibility and control because here the floor supports the entire body and eliminates the stresses of gravity and weight.

A child receives information coming directly from the action of the muscles and joints. This is called kinesthesis and/or proprioception and is important to the individual's awareness of muscle actions. It is thus the individual can know which muscles are performing, and what this performance is accomplishing. When a child is lying flat on the floor, without the need to hold self erect and in balance to avoid falling, fullest attention can be given to the movements being explored. Likewise, full attention can be given to NOT moving--to how muscles can be turned off and relaxed. Here is an opportunity for the "hyperactive" child to experience "*hypo*activity" and *im*mobility. This can be the beginning of the sensitivity to minute muscle control. Since previous editions of this book, the Angels in the Snow procedure has been widely used by both standard and special classroom pupils with excellent results. Many teachers and adaptive physical education specialists have reported the improvements noted in the children who had daily opportunity to practice both movement control for mobility and the relaxation for immobility. An improvement in handwriting has been a frequently reported gain, but gains in total coordination, and a noticeable reduction of distractability have also been reported by a number of educators. Again, it stands to reason when a child can control and synchronize body movements in one routine, there is a greater possibility of achieving movement efficiencies in other action patterns. After all, a child is a *total action system*.[50,56,53]

There are a great number of routines which might be included here. All of these can be helpful in the acquisition of body-muscle awareness (called *body scheme*) and to the enhancement of all the movements available to the human. Since the goal of this book is to guide each child through the activities which provide exploration and integration of the movement abilities closely related to the learning process, the few routines given are examples, and parents should use their own imagination for more routines. A good exercise book will provide other procedures, and most of these are recommended because too many children are too inactive and unfamiliar with the movements available to them for the development of efficient, directed actions which will then develop good body schemes. These opportunities for children to develop movement skills should start early in infancy. Probably the best of all books for parents is *Playful Parenting* by Grasselli and Hegner, and should be obtained by every parent of a first child, then used for all following children.

b. Flexibility and Postural Balance

All previous editions of this book gave considerable attention to routines which resembled exercises for strength and bulk of muscles. There is now ample evidence that more attention must be given to those procedures which contribute to body flexibility and postural balance. The human is a combination of architectural halves and the ultimate unity of these halves will be the basis for poise and grace in movement; for the greatest readiness to move quickly, efficiently and effectively in response to a personal need. The routines here, then, are chosen to help the child find how all movements are related to balance and accuracy of movement. Thus, the relatedness and integrations of body parts can be achieved.

Roll and Rise, from Back to Hands and Knees

Have your child lie supine (face up) with legs straight and arms at the sides. At your signal, your child is to roll over and rise to hands and knees, facing the floor. Next, have him roll back to the supine position on the floor. At the next signal, have your child roll to the opposite side and rise again to hands and knees. This routine utilizes arm thrust for rolling and rising but also includes the appropriate leg actions to reach the final position. Here the legs are used to assist the roll and a coordination of arms, torso and legs is developed.

Roll and Rise, from Back to Hands and Feet

This routine is much like the previous one except the child now must come to an "all-fours" position instead of the hands and knees creeping posture. Further, legs must be kept straight and there must be more bending at the hips and waist. This routine will assist in developing hip and waist flexibility in preparation for the next routine and for the rotational flexibility so essential to proper walking patterns.

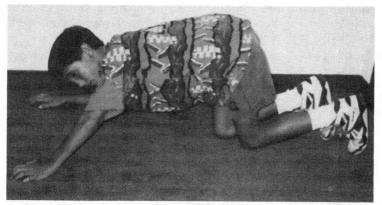

Figure 11. Roll and Rise actions bring body flexibility and arm and leg thrusts that lead to total coordination.

Rolling Sit-ups

Once again have your child lie on the floor, face downward. Have him place hands on the floor, palms downward as if doing push-ups. When you say "go," the child is to roll to the back and up into a sitting position, using hands and arms to give the thrust needed to raise the upper body. If the roll is to the left, the right arm should push into the roll and both arms should then push into the sitting position. Next, have your child roll to the right to find what both arms must do to complete the sit-up. Remember to have your child use the words "right" or "left" as the rolls are made for the added practice in the words and concepts of directionality.

When there is observable flexibility and coordination achieved, have your child roll to either right or left, but continue rolling until the prone, face down position is again reached. These rolling sit-ups and full rolls develop a combination of arm thrusts and lift with torso twists to bring greater awareness of body positions and directions of movement. Verbalizing the directions of movement gives practice in the language that will become the expression of many directions of movements.

In the previous paragraphs much emphasis has been given to the importance of the visual system as the "steersman" for all general movement activities. Most of the routines just described give little opportunity for the visual system to do this steering and appraising of one's performance. The moment any activity is introduced which moves the child away from a limited area of action, the visual steering factor MUST be included in the practice routines. Any time a child moves across the room or across any space, the visual awareness and the visual judgments of the surroundings must be a definite part of the action. The child who has not learned to use vision to direct his movements has not learned to be an observant individual and will miss information from many of those things in his surrounding world. This is the child who too frequently hears an adult saying, "Why don't you look where you are going?" The next routine will help this child in learning to "look where he is going." At the same time, it will help this child in learning to "read" all those signs that are the pertinent symbols for patterns of action in our busy world.

c. Obstacle Course

There has already been comment about the importance of creeping as an important contributor to the interweaving and coordination of body sides and the actions of the extremities. These creeping actions are preliminaries for running and skipping as well as for walking. The experienced track coach knows that arm thrusts are important to the totality of body and leg movements for the sprinter. There are many advanced exercises designed to develop this arm-body-legs unity and reciprocity. The older children who, for some reason or another, cannot participate in the advanced routines of the athletic coach, may resist creeping activities as being too childish and embarrassing. An obstacle course, devised as follows, can appeal to most children and will demand many of the body movements which should have been explored during the pre-walking months of infancy.

Using your child's own flat hands, feet and knees as the patterns, draw around these on light-weight white cardboard. Cut out many of these forms so you will have enough of them to make "tracks" around the house. Arrange these "prints" so your child must creep under tables, then walk across the room, and then creep across an adjoining room. The patterns can be taped to the floor with masking tape and can be fastened to davenports and rugs with straight pins. With a bit of imagination parents can place "tracks" through the entire house--baby steps, giant steps, walking backward and frontward; up and down stairs backward and frontward; with more variation than can be given here. The "prints" can be used over and over again and will justify the time involved in making them.

A more advanced sort of obstacle course can easily be devised by using furniture instead of the cutouts of footprints and handprints. Arrange furniture so it is accessible for climbing over it, under it or around it, in every possible manner. Give your child verbal instructions on the pieces of furniture to be used and the sequence in which these are to be used. Children having difficulty with *sequencing* may have to be given one instruction at a time. Others can take two or three instructions and carry them out. Ask your child to repeat your instructions *before* moving into the course. Again, verbalization by you as an auditory signal for the child and the verbalization before acting is a review and reinforcement for practice in *sequencing*. Here every sort of body movement is required for "running the course" and giving your child a time challenge can encourage him to extend the ability to complete the course you have devised. There are no limits to the possibilities in an obstacle course, and devising one for a playground area can become a neighborhood benefit.

Postural balance and bilaterality of body sides and extremities are closely related. In fact, good balance in posture and movement is a product of this body bilaterality. After your child has developed the abilities discussed above, it is important there be an extension of these newly gained skills into activities that will further enhance the integration of vision and movement.

d. Rebounders

All previous editions of this book discussed trampolines with rules and procedures. Trampolines have many clinical advantages and can be found in the therapy rooms of many behavioral optometrists, where there are specific procedures to develop general bilaterality as a preliminary to ocular bilaterality. Once again, the goal is for the general organization which will lead to special coordinations and integrations with vision as the directing agent. All this is much better achieved under the cautious and judicious supervision of the optometrist or the fully qualified optometric therapist. There is no intent that this device be used to build gymnastic abilities. Instead, the trampoline provides a very special situation in which visually directed movement MUST occur or the participant will not master this elastic surface. Although it has clinical advantages not available elsewhere, it is not as procurable as it was a few years ago. Rebounders, like those now on display in every sporting goods store, can be useful and beneficial in building the basic patterns of visually directed movement. The rebounder, usable in almost any room in the house, allows a child to move from the floor procedures just described to the postural balance routines while in erect posture.

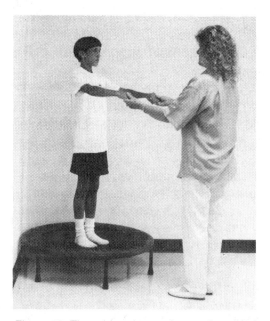

Figure 12. The rebounder can be used anywhere and provides practice in postural balance and coordination not achieved in any other activity. This device is much more than an exerciser and should be available to every preschool child.

Although the rebounder is quite safe for use by a child of any

50

age, there are a few simple rules to be followed.

1. There should be only one child at a time on the rebounder.

2. Sneakers or tennis shoes should be worn if the rebounder has a nylon bed. If the bed is canvas or rubber coated, the child should jump in bare feet.

3. The rebounder is to be used to achieve coordination of the two sides of the body, coordination of arms with legs, and for balance and body flexibility. Therefore, NO tricks should be attempted during any of the routines suggested here.

Rhythm

Help your child to find a rhythm of bouncing in which there is the exploration of how arm actions do assist in continuing the action. As soon as some fluidity of movement is noted, have your child bounce to your measured, rhythmic counting, and then to music which has a march or country tempo. Rhythm of movement is extremely important to efficiency of movement, and this is more easily achieved on the rebounder than it is in any other activity. Further, the attraction of the rebounder encourages a child to practice and to achieve a sense of rhythm. Several authorities have now shown that the child who has not learned rhythm by the age of 3 will have some difficulties in school, where counting, writing, singing and choral speaking all require a sense of rhythm.[54]

A fair substitute for the trampoline or rebounder can be devised as follows: Obtain two discarded, but unbroken, coil bed springs and a cotton pad mattress. The springs are placed one on top of the other and wired together so they will stay one on the other. The mattress is then placed on top of the springs. This furnishes a bed-sized jumping surface upon which any child can learn the fundamentals of jumping. The device can be placed in basement playrooms or on the ground in the backyard. It is also suitable for classrooms with low ceilings.

Body Twists and Rotations

Here is another splendid opportunity for the verbalization of the direction words, right and left, as the turn is anticipated. Since too many watches are now digital models, children are not learning the full meaning of the words *clockwise* and *counterclockwise*. These are still important words for the language of directionality that our culture uses for more than the movements of clock hands. Here, again, the rebounder provides an opportunity for concept development that is not available elsewhere. Urge your child to start at 12 o'clock and land facing 3 o'clock, facing 6 o'clock, 9 o'clock, and each hour represented by the numbers on a clock face. Such movements will bring strong influences upon both time and space concepts, and every child should have such opportunities to do more than memorize a clock face.

Start and Stop

The ability to stop movement has been discussed. The rebounder offers the experience in which control of hips, knees and feet all participate in the act of stopping the action. Urge your child to stop on the count of four, or any other number chosen, and work until both starts and stops are matched to the numbers chosen. Counting to four, for example, and stopping on five is not acceptable since there should be the learned anticipation of the act of stopping *before* reaching the number four. Learning how to get ready to stop is as important as actually learning to stop, and the very young child needs extra practice here to get the fullest appreciation of what numbers are for and how they can be used. This routine assists every child to match his voice to the bounce. Many children who have not achieved a sense of rhythm and the concepts of sequence have great difficulty counting their steps as they walk across a room. Counting bounces and vocally adding numbers to the action enhances both rhythm and sequence. This should be a daily practice routine for the child having *any* difficulty in kindergarten or first grade.[54]

Directionality

Numerous references have been made to concepts of directionality and ways to achieve these concepts. It is now a well established fact that children who are having "reversals" are also having problems with directionality in many other situations. We must remember that the directions of hand movement proper for making each letter are a cultural essential and just have to be mastered by the child in the introductions to the alphabet. There will be a much more detailed discussion of this in the next section, but the concepts expressed by the words for directions (right and left) need to be mastered *before* the child is introduced to the classroom tasks which demand a full understanding of these words and many more direction words. Since these are strictly cultural impositions, early practice in what the words mean can be singularly important to every child. It is now known that the child who arrives in school with concepts of right and left fully established does not struggle with the reversals problem.[71,44,50,68,72]

Every possible opportunity should be found to have your child use these labels (left or right) as he moves about the house. When you ask your child to find something, emphasize that it is "in the *right hand* corner of your closet," or "you will find it in the top *left hand* drawer of your desk." Use these words in every way you can so they become as common to your child's experiences and language development as any other words you use to communicate information.

Should your child continue to have difficulty with directions at the end of kindergarten, a simple floor maze can be most helpful and a very challenging game. If you have a garage, or carport, with a clean floor, make the maze pattern with masking tape as illustrated in Figure 13. Or, using heavy string, lay out a similar pattern on the floor of the family room, pinning the corners so they will stay in place while your child walks the maze.

Have your child start at one end of the maze and walk the pattern slowly. He must tell whether a right or left turn will be made at each corner *before* arriving at the corner. As soon as the turns can be named without hesitation, have your child start at the other end of the maze so the corners are now new.

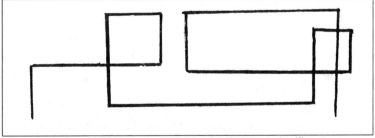

Figure 13. The masking tape maze can be the most significant contributor to concepts of directionality. Here all the mysteries of "right" and "left" can be mastered before the classroom tasks can create any confusions or "reversals."

When you are confident mastery of these directions has been achieved, have your child walk someone else through the pattern. In this activity, your child must call the turns *as if* he were in the action and must visualize and anticipate what another individual must do to complete the maze. If your child says "right" on a left corner, follow the instructions so your child's mistake is illustrated by your "running off the road." Again, your child's instructions MUST be given before you reach the corner, or your turning will be a clue he, or she, will depend upon. This can be made into a game where the "walker" gets the privilege of being the "caller" if a mistake is made. The challenge lies in finding which player can get the other person through the maze first without a mistake at any corner. This may seem to be a very simple activity but it is closely related to map reading in geography and to the directions one must give another to get him *from* his house *to* your house. The eventual skill is the full mastery of reversibility wherein one always knows that many words can be purposefully reversed for other meanings, and that objects which face us will be in a rotated position. Classroom reversals are only a problem when this skill of reversibility is not achieved.

All Playground Activities

Children's needs for many more directed general movement activities cannot be overemphasized. Too many children are leading a sedentary existence, with much too much time spent sitting in front of a television set. All the negatives of this need not be repeated here. Since children are now hauled almost everywhere they go, all running and throwing games should be made available to them. Swimming is one of the very best activities for the development of total body integrations of the directed movement patterns. Many specific activities could be listed here, but alert, informed parents will encourage their children to participate in the neighborhood playground programs. All of these lay the critically important foundations for the more specialized movement patterns we will now be discussing. As has been frequently implied, the sequence of these activities is important and it is most important your child finds how, when and why the visual system assists in all of the visual-spatial decisions which are gathering more and more significance in our rapidly moving culture.

There have been numerous clinical studies and researches which prove that postural balance, fluent bilaterality, and all of the movement skills which evolve, make significant contributions to intellectual development. The contributions of Montessori in the early 1900s, the elaborate benchmark studies of infant and child development by Gesell in the '30s and '40s, the insightful observation of Piaget in the '40s and '50s, and the more recent laboratory research of Smith and Smith all show, beyond any doubt, that the developmental interweavings of movement in the human have a direct influence upon both physical and cognitive potentials. One of the most complete studies was conducted by the Texas State Department of Health and the Texas State Department of Education under the direction of a man named Harmon in 1942 and 1943. At that time, 160,000 elementary school children were carefully appraised with clinical attention to the visual, nutritional, dental, postural and general health status of each child. Changes were then made in the classroom environments which would enhance both the general and special movement abilities of each child. These changes included improved lighting, improved wall and chalkboard colors, better temperature controls, and most significant, more comfortable seating while studying. Desks with properly sloped working surface, which were completely adjustable to the size of every child, were provided. The results of this extensive study, shown here in Figure 14, seem to have been lost in the preoccupation with academic scores--which have not been all that good these past 10 or 15 years! It is difficult to comprehend why the individual child's well-being in the inherently stressful learning situation has been so completely overlooked since this study was completed. There has been a blind rush to introduce the Three R's whether or not the child is developmentally ready for these academic tasks. It only takes a brief visit to any primary classroom to observe large children in small desks, and small children in big desks, all of whom are experiencing movement restrictions which multiply various health problems and academic frustrations to the point of failure.[18,28,52,29,55,35,40,41]

Unfortunately, the American educational system is no longer very approachable, and parents cannot have the direct influence they had in times past where the system would quickly respond to parental concerns. Since the modern classroom is designed more for ad-

COMPARISON OF SOME HEALTH PROBLEMS FOUND AT BEGINNING AND END OF THE SIX-MONTH EXPERIMENTAL PERIOD
November, 1942 and May, 1943
Becker School, Austin, Texas

PROBLEM	Percent of cases found in November 1942	Percent of cases found in May 1943	Percentage change during six-month period
Visual Difficulties	53.3	18.6	-65.0
Nutrition Problems	71.3	37.2	-47.8
Chronic Infection	75.2	42.6	-43.3
Posture Problems.	30.2	22.4	-25.6
Chronic Fatigue.	20.9	9.3	-55.6

*Children entering school after November, 1942 eliminated from this table.

COMPARISON OF VISUAL DIFFICULTIES FOUND AT BEGINNING AND END OF THE SIX-MONTH EXPERIMENTAL PERIOD
November, 1942 and May, 1943
Becker School, Austin, Texas
Shown Graphically in Figure 20

GRADE LEVEL	Percent of cases found in November 1942	Percent of cases found in May 1943*	Percentage change during six-month period
ENTIRE SCHOOL	53.3	18.6	-65.0
Grade 1A	30.7	7.6	-75.0
Grade 1B	35.7	21.4	-40.0
Grade 2A	38.4	23.0	-40.0
Grade 2B	46.1	23.0	-50.0
Grade 3A	58.3	8.3	-85.7
Grade 3B	61.5	15.3	-75.0
Grade 4A	66.6	20.0	-70.0
Grade 4B	72.7	27.2	-62.5
Grade 5A	71.4	21.4	-70.0

*Children entering school after November, 1942 eliminated from this table.

Figure 14. Statistical results of classroom environment changes which had almost immediate benefits for children in the primary grades. This study has been repeated several times with very similar positive results.

ACHIEVEMENT GROWTH BY MONTHS OF EDUCATIONAL AGE DURING THE SIX-MONTH EXPERIMENTAL PERIOD

November, 1942 to May, 1943

Becker School, Austin, Texas

	Range of growth	Mean change	Median change	Model change	Percent changing 6 mo. or less	Percent changing less than 6 mo.	Percent changing 6 mo. only	Percent changing over 6 mo.
	Months	Months	Months	Months				
Experimental School	0-32	10.2	10.0	10.0	24.0	16.6	7.4	76.0
Grade 1A	0-18	9.8	9.0	9.0	25.0	18.7	6.3	75.0
Grade 1B	0-21	10.8	11.5	10.5	14.2	14.2	0.0	85.8
Grade 2A	4-19	10.9	9.0	8.3	9.0	6.0	3.0	91.0
Grade 2B	4-17	9.4	9.0	9.0	26.6	20.0	6.6	73.4
Grade 3A	6-24	11.7	11.0	10.9	10.5	0.0	10.5	89.5
Grade 3B	2-32	13.5	14.5	14.5	16.6	11.1	5.5	83.4
Grade 4A	5-25	10.9	10.0	10.0	15.3	7.6	7.7	84.7
Grade 4B	4-27	11.8	12.0	11.0	26.3	21.0	5.3	73.7
Grade 5A	3-15	8.9	10.0	11.0	24.1	20.6	3.5	75.9
Control School	-8 to +18	6.8	6.0	6.0	66.6	44.4	22.2	33.4

Figure 15. The reduction of health problems brings 76% gains in educational age while the control group only experienced a 33% gain. Good health means good academic progress.

ministrative convenience than it is for children's best health, it really falls to parents to arrange home study centers for the most productive and easiest homework. There are basic rules which will guide parents in the arrangements for this home study center.

The height of your child's desk and chair will determine the amount of fatigue your child may have. When these are the proper size for your child, they will also allow the postural movements for longer study time. The following illustrations show how to determine the proper desk height for your child. The inclined work surface, as illustrated, makes a flat table into a sloped surface most appropriate for postural balance and comfort. This sloped surface also assures less fatiguing visual situations, and was the most significant of all the changes made in the Texas study.[55,35] (See Figures 16,17.)

The proper chair height can be determined by having your child sit on the chair he is to use, with both feet on the floor. In this position you should be able to barely slip your flat hand under his thighs just behind his knees. This will give him the support he needs without the leg strangulation which will occur if his feet do not touch the floor. If, in contrast, the chair is too low, and his weight is thrown back on the point of his buttocks, there will be discomfort and wriggling, with less ability to stay at his homework. If this is the situation, you will be able to put your entire hand under his thighs just behind his knees. If this seat is too low, you will either have to find a chair with legs of proper length, or use pillows to raise your child (see Figure 18).

If you have had the opportunity to visit a classroom lately, you will probably have observed children writing on paper or in their workbooks while these are placed without any of the rotation that also prevents fatigue. Too frequently the paper or book is placed straight in front of a child with edges parallel to desk edges. This improper placement is what causes the left-handed child to hook his pencil hand so he can see what he is writing. A very simple rotation of the paper, as shown in Figures 19 and 20, will allow both the left- and right-handed children to sit up in a much more comfortable and balanced posture instead of the very undesirable head-almost-on-desk posture too often seen. This rotation of the

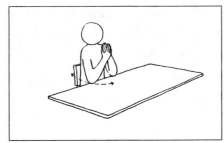

Figure 16. Desk height can be determined by laying one palm over the other as illustrated here. When your child swings his arms, his elbows should just clear the front edge of the table.

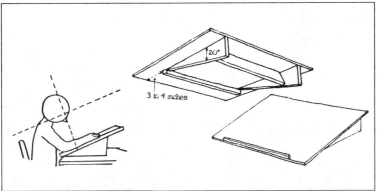

3 to 4 inches

20°

Figure 17. The sloped study surface can be easily made as illustrated here. The surface area can vary from 14 to 24 inches deep and 24 to 36 inches wide, depending upon the size of the table at which your child will be studying. An overhang of the front edge of two to four inches will permit your child easier access to the working surface. Cover the contact points of the supports with felt to prevent marring the table upon which this working surface is placed.

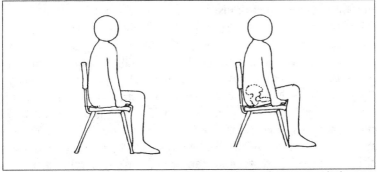

Figure 18. The illustration on the left above shows the proper chair height. The illustration on the right shows how discomfort comes from a chair too low.

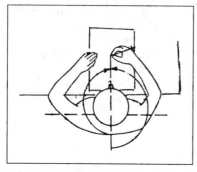

Figure 19. This illustrates the usual, but incorrect, placement of the paper or workbook in front of a child. This situation creates fatigue which then reduces comprehension and productivity.

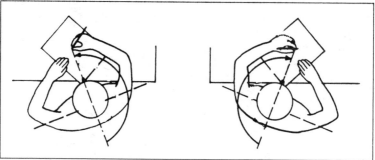

Figure 20. The proper rotations of paper and workbook are illustrated here for both the right- and left-handed child. These paper positions can prevent the hooked left hand and the excessive fatigue even in the right-handed child.

paper was all that had to be added to the Texas study to reduce the incidence of back problems and dental malocclusions.[35]

Before this discussion of general movement patterns and general welfare is closed, there must be a comment about nutrition. Your behavioral optometrist is fully aware of nutritional balances and their significance to academic performance. The contemporary optometrist, who gives special attention to the totality of human performance, has more carefully studied nutrition than have many other clinicians. Many young patients demonstrate visual difficulties which are positively modified when diet is improved and maintained. Thus, nutrition is a factor given careful consideration in many optometric offices. If, by any chance, parents are not also fully aware of these factors, the optometrist will refer them to nutritional authorities for full information and guidance on how to best serve a school child's needs.[73]

B—SPECIAL MOVEMENT PATTERNS
(Procedures for the development of manipulative skills)

The human being possesses a pair of tools that are unequaled anywhere else in nature. These are the hands, and they provide us with the machinery for the manipulation and discriminating contact exploration of nearly all of his productivity. There are many stories about people who have learned to take care of themselves with their feet and toes, but there are no real substitutes for the hands. The very best of the artificial arms and hands give the user a limited replacement of the hands.

Studies of prehistoric mankind now show that the hands, steered by the eyes and vision, account for most of the progress of civilization. The extended studies of the human infant also show the importance of the hands in his growth and development toward productive individuality. Although there are many special movement patterns that a child must master, the eye-hand patterns are chronologically and developmentally most significant. Gesell states, "The infant takes hold of the world with his eyes long before he takes hold with his hands." This is undoubtedly true, but full performance and comprehension of "the world" cannot come until the eyes and hands are used in unified combination to probe and minutely explore "the world." A child must have the opportunities to "*feel* what things *see* like--and to *see* what things *feel* like." (From "Vision, Its Development in Infant and Child," by Getman and Streff. New York, Harper and Brothers, 1949, and from "Mommy and Daddy--You Can Help Me Learn to See," published by the Women's Auxiliary to the American Optometric Association, 243 N. Lindbergh Blvd., St. Louis, MO, 1959.)

Too frequently parents unthinkingly prevent the opportunities that give a child eye-hand practice. Many household objects and knick-knacks are verboten and parents attempt to substitute thoroughly explored and familiar toys for all of the "no-no" attractions. Every child has a driving desire to explore the likenesses and differences that exist in the objects around him. The valuable or dangerous objects should be put out of sight and reach, but even some breakage is essential to a full understanding of the world.

Parents make another gross mistake in the selection of their child's objects for learning play. They will give a child toys or games that are too difficult for his level of eye-hand dexterity, and then wonder why their child is not interested in any of the playthings they have provided. A child's interest in any object stems from its usefulness to him. Just because it is attractive to an adult does not assure its attractiveness to a child.

It Is Easy To Please A Child

I brought my daughter the kind of doll
A parent is proud to bring.
She opened her toy with cries of joy
... and played all day with the string!

She said she wanted to build a house
So I got her a set of blocks.
The present, I guess, was a great success
... She built a house with the box!

Because it hurt me to see her weep
when I made an issue of it,
I bought her a game, and when it came
... she played with the tissue of it!

C. S. Jennison

Playthings should always be learning things, and the learning factor must be assured by the provision of objects that fit the child's level of visual-manual development. Thus, the child's development of special movement patterns will be assured.

1. A percolator is one of the most important "toys" a child can have. Its uses are unlimited. It is a simplified, yet more all-inclusive, model of nested pieces. It provides eye-hand experience in shapes, sizes, textures, temperature, inside or outside, curved or flat, top or bottom, light or heavy (when empty or filled), and is very durable. Observation of many children has shown that the percolator is the toy that holds a child's interest throughout the preschool years. It goes with the child from the crib to the sandbox and bathtub, to the lake, and even to kindergarten.

2. Every child should have his own cupboard or drawer in the kitchen. A toy chest in the nursery is a nice piece of furniture and serves a purpose in teaching a child to put his toys away. Most young children spend many hours in the kitchen because their mothers spend so many hours there. A cupboard or drawer of his own becomes his treasure chest and will save Mother many steps. Most important of all, this treasure chest provides visual search and manual reach opportunities not found elsewhere.

3. Many so-called educational toys are very valuable, but they are also too difficult for the young child. Most manufacturers are now placing age-level tags on their products. It is still the parents' responsibility to choose the educational toy that is best suited to their own child's manipulative abilities. Furthermore, some of the popular toys fail to give a child the visual clues that match the manual clues. For example, Tinker Toys use a round piece for a square corner. This is not to say that Tinker Toys are unimportant to the older child. The point here is that a child should have the opportunity to make square corners out of square materials before he moves to round-square corners. Experience with truly square corners first will make the use of Tinker Toys and Erector Sets more productive later. Many children who have been given these advanced games before their eye-hand skills were adequately developed lost all the pieces before their values were fully appreciated. In such instances, parents have said, "Oh, he had one of those and never used it, so we never replaced it."

The best toy available at the present time is LEGO. The infant's set is called DUPLO, and both of these should be available to every child. There are now numerous imitations of LEGO and all of these are excellent, but LEGO provides the most possibilities for imaginative play. Here the child will have all the visual tactual experiences which follow the child's ability to build from the instructions in the guide book to the expansion of inventiveness and creativeness which will come out of the child's own designs. These valuable materials provide color, size, shape, position and block fitting experiences which are completely unique, and which should be encouraged for all possible pastime play.

There is a little secret that parents have found to make all toys more valuable. When a child seems to become tired of a particular toy it should be put out of sight and reach for a period of time. When the child asks for it after several weeks or months, it emerges as a "new" toy with new interest in it. This rotation of toys encourages a child to make better use of fewer toys and there will be much less scatter of those toys with which the child is not playing.

4. Every father who is a "weekend carpenter" is aware of the desire his children exhibit to use hammer and nails. These children should be given a scrap of soft lumber, a light-weight hammer and short nails with large heads so they can "carpenter," too. The nails should be started for them to avoid the pounded fingers that might discourage this activity. The integration of hand movements and dexterity with visual steering and control of eye fixations makes this activity valuable to the child's total development. It is also very useful in the development of special movement patterns of hands and eyes.

5. Permit your child to use his preferred hand. If he seems to be ambidextrous, help him to gain a preferred hand after determining by observation which hand is most frequently used. Also watch him to see which hand he seems to control better in all special movements. Do not insist that he always uses just one hand in simple activities. There is more and more evidence in the study of handedness that rigid unilaterality can also be a handicap to a child. Many occupational activities demand that both hands be in alternate or supporting action.

Help your child to gain the use of either hand in actions where either hand can serve him well. Two-handed skills are just as important as the single-hand skills.

6. Although many references have been made here to the value of bilateral and reciprocal interweaving of the two halves of the body, it is almost impossible to place too much emphasis upon it. The more development in bilaterality that your child achieves, the more chance he has of being able to do many things well. It is now a known fact that many chronic ailments result from the lack of freedom in bilaterality. Harmon[36] has shown that dental

problems and communicable illnesses (as well as visual problems) are more prevalent in the children who lack full freedom of movements in both halves of their body. Activities such as Jacks, Lincoln Logs, Tinker Toys, swings, wheelbarrows, tricycles and bicycles are aids to the child in gaining advanced coordination.

7. Tracing around blocks and cutouts or tracing the outlines of simple, heavy line pictures is excellent practice for your child. It furnishes a definite visual pattern for the child to follow while allowing freedom of direction and mobility of hand. It also creates a need to use the non-preferred hand in a supportive role while it holds the pattern to be traced.

8. Many fathers are upset and concerned about a child's inability to catch a ball tossed to him. Catch should be played with balloons before catch with a ball is attempted. The balloon floats slowly enough for the child to learn control of hands and fingers necessary for speedy grasp in catching it as it comes to him through the air. Large, round, slow balloons should be used first, then smaller balloons, and finally large, heavier beach balls will provide the skills of hands and eyes essential to catching softballs and baseballs. Here it is again important to remind all parents that skills with a baseball glove--a one-handed act--must evolve from basic bilaterality which originates from catching the balloons.

9. Cut out simple forms. When the child wishes to cut out pictures, encourage him to start by cutting out the "picture of a picture"--by following simple lines that encircle the picture. For example, it will be very helpful to him to have black crayon lines shaped like a picture frame around his picture of a dog, truck or baby. This allows him to cut out pictures by keeping the directions of his scissors simple and within his ability. As his cutting skill increases, the crayon lines can be drawn closer to the contour of the actual picture. Thus, his skill increases with the increasing complexity of the task, until he no longer needs the crayon outlines and can cut on the actual picture lines. This develops the highly important eye-hand skills wherein the visual judgments are the specific guides to hand activities.

10. Have your child fit objects together, nested cubes of various sizes, simple jigsaw puzzles, etc. Many of the cans that are discarded from the kitchen can be prepared so that nested sizes can be obtained. Duplicate this activity for older children by having them stack dishes, set the table, sort silverware, etc.

11. A most interesting toy is the one called LITEBRITE. This is a lighted pegboard and any child will enjoy following the patterns included with the toy, and then creating new patterns and pictures. This toy provides colored plastic pegs through which the light shines for accent and variety. If the patterns included are too difficult, cut familiar shapes (squares, circles and triangles) of various sizes out of light cardboard and place these on the front of the LITEBRITE so the pegs can be inserted to outline the pattern. As soon as dexterity and accurate visual tactual skills are apparent, have your child outline shapes using those holes that are one, two, or even three spaces away from the cardboard patterns. Ask your child to critique the peg placements. Are the lines straight where they should be straight? Are the corners the proper angles? What are the similarities and differences between the cardboard patterns and the peg patterns? All of this provides visual tactual activities followed by the visual inspections for comparisons. As the ability to make pictures on this toy increases, urge your child to use fewer pegs to make the outlines. When he or she can illustrate a square by placing only four pegs in the proper corner positions, there is the emergence of the ability to perceive form while using minimal clues. This is known as *visual closure*, and becomes very important to the visual interpretation of pictures and diagrams in textbooks.

12. Have your child trace shapes, his name and other simple words with crayon or pencil, using carbon paper or magic slates. Lift the paper and see how accurate is his tracing. This allows visual comparison and helps to develop the ability to make visual discrimination of likes and differences. Repeat until the tracing is as near like the original as possible. Then have your child copy his name or the simple words without tracing.

This section on special movement patterns cannot be closed

without more discussion of movements that are truly very special and unique in man. These are the movements and dexterities of hands. The hands of man are one of God's masterpieces and are totally unmatched for the abilities and skills an individual can develop here. The behavioral optometrist is justifiably entranced with the structure and function of the two eyes--and all of the synchrony which must exist in the visual system for its ultimate performance. Although the visual system and all of its movements, which will be discussed in the next section, is the supreme receiver of information, and the dominant input system for cognition, the hands must be recognized as the supreme action system for the output that follows visual discriminations and decisions. Hundreds of books have been written about the wonders of the human hand and its myriad dexterities. At the risk of redundancy here, there must be some comments, which may, hopefully, alert parents to some of the hard facts about their children's inadequacies in these special movement skills required for the exploration and manipulation of the contents of this world.

Frequent references have been made here about the relationships existing between hands and eyes--vision and taction. This is so much more than the ability to beat PacMan or any other video game and is so critical to the mastery of the computers now being thrust into kindergarten and first grade classroom, that this organization of the visual and the tactual systems needs some explanation. It will be additionally considered in later sections and this discussion here can be preparation for what is to come.[67]

Renshaw was quoted earlier as saying that: "Vision develops under the tutelage of the *active* touch." The word "active" has been italicized here to emphasize that Renshaw was referring to dexterity. At first glance, this statement may seem quite esoteric, and can raise confusing questions--until one considers all of the visual decisions which can be made out of a background of *active* tactual experiences. The human usually makes interpretations of sizes, shapes, textures, temperatures, solidities and weights by visually inspecting things. The fact remains, no matter how many visual inspections are made, none of these judgments will be accurate unless there have been previous tactual explorations and manipulations of those things having one or more of these characteristics.

Again, it has been redundantly said, the young child spends most of his preschool years looking and feeling, feeling and looking, in the quest for the skill that allows the visual system to make these judgments without needing to return to tactual manipulations for the information being sought. Thus, the hand/finger dexterities which come out of all these manipulations provide the tutelage Renshaw said the visual system needed. The developmental need for this exploratory experience is so great, and so often missed, there are now too many children arriving at the classroom door with severe deficiencies in the abilities God intended the hands to have.[25]

Toys and tools have already been suggested as the experiences which allow a child to find out what hands are for. All of these activities can assist the child to manipulate and master the real things he will find in the world. The classroom puts a tremendously different demand upon a child's hands. Suddenly he finds he is expected to use crayons and pencils as his "tools" in the activities which do not have the same concrete realness. Parents need to be aware of the complexity of the sudden shift from realities to abstractions, and the hand skills a child must have for success in this move to symbols. Now there are needs for tactual and visual abilities not previously acquired by many children. Too many preschool toys are already assembled and have only buttons to press. Too many preschool activities are so structured for the child there is little opportunity for the manipulative experiences the child should be having.

Some of the most effective guidance routines thus far devised for the development of all these hand-eye coordinations the child will need in the classroom require nothing more than a large chalkboard and the child's use of it. In the intervening years since chalkboards were suggested in previous editions there has been ample evidence of their value. Children find this surface to be a source of both pleasure and creativity. Here, mistakes are not the problem they are when a sheet of paper is "spoiled." Parents have reported their children spending many hours at drawing and the early writing activities at the chalkboard. Teachers are reporting that handwriting and spelling improve almost immediately, and detailed suggestions for these improvements will be given in the next section. The preschool child finds the chalkboard fascinating and does much of his early scribbling on it. Several young mothers have reported their children no longer draw on the wallpaper when a chalkboard is at their disposal. Most children need to scribble. Scribbling is visually and psychologically beneficial because it gives the child a visible pattern of the movements his hand has just made. The chalkboard should be used in some manner as a preliminary to every school assignment, and parents will find students using it through the high school years as a place to get the mistakes made and the details cleared before putting it all on paper.

The home chalkboard should be at least four feet wide and wider if there is space for it in the child's room, the playroom, or in a garage area. Such a size is difficult to obtain and is commercially expensive. A splendid chalkboard can be made by obtaining a full 4' x 8' sheet of masonite, or hardboard, at the lumber yard. This can be painted with a chalkboard paint which will give it the finely textured surface it should have. This paint is now available in spray cans and comes under the brand name of Zonylite. The surface this particular type of paint produces is much better than the surface of the very slick, white, message boards upon which a felt tip pen is used. Although the yellow railroad chalk for the chalkboard is dusty, there is the *feel* of the movements not available on the white boards.

This green, textured surface should not be washed. Good erasers and soft cloths will pick up the dust and allow the corrections desired. If this surface is washed with soap and water, it will soon lose the very surface texture that makes it so beneficial to the *looks and the feel* of whatever is chalked upon it.

There is one aspect of the wall chalkboard as a training and guidance device which must be noted here. The erect posture which is unique to the human being is achieved after 12-14 months of practice and experience in all the general movements of infancy. Thus, a chalkboard hung on a wall provides a surface for performance that is most available to a child because it contributes to, and matches, the child's concepts of directionality which have evolved in the processes of gaining the erect posture. This erect posture frees the arms and hands so they may become the tools of performance.

Standing at the chalkboard enhances the freedom of arm and hand movements. The vertical plane of the board is conducive to full arm movements with the child's shoulder as the primary pivot for vertical, horizontal and diagonal lines. The elbow and wrist enter into the action for the extension and retraction of the hand as it moves over the chalkboard surface. Wrist rotations and finger motions in holding and manipulating the chalk complete the full sequence from gross whole arm to distinct finger control.

Many children have great difficulty learning to write and their efforts to do so are full of stress and muscular tensions. Their first "words on paper" are scribbles, but the writing of the older child need not continue to be the scribble that so many high school and college instructors are presently having to decipher and interpret. We must again remember that our species is structured and designed for erect postures. Writing surfaces such as desks and tables are cultural in origin and only in very recent years have they been adapted to a child's body mechanics.

The use of the chalkboard as described here will greatly assist in overcoming the counter stresses of the desk surfaces. When the pattern of movement for writing a word is established in the entire arm, the child's writing becomes smoother and more legible before the "scribble" is established as a habit.

Retarded children have provided us with another bit of interesting information. They have particularly illustrated that children learn "up" and "down" quite well, and with ease, when it is expressed by their own hand or body movements. "Top and "bottom" are learned through activities with objects, toys and furniture. All of these they can transfer to the vertical surface of the chalkboard.

The difficulty arises in the 90 degree rotation necessary to recognize the "top" of a sheet of paper on the desk as being the edge farthest from them. Frequently when children are asked to draw a line on the top of a sheet, they place it anywhere on the sheet and insist it has been drawn "on the top" because it is the topside surface. When instructed to draw a line at the bottom of the page, they will turn the paper over because "bottom" is "underneath" or is the "down" side! Repetition of instruction and explanation of top and bottom and drill on paper may not resolve the problem for them. Their concept of top and bottom has come from their experience in movements; it is not the same as the adult cultural concept, and they have no feeling (kinesthesis) for it in their developmental background. The use of the chalkboard on the wall, followed by its use while slanted at 45 degrees, or on an easel, has cleared this problem so very well that it should almost be routine for all children.

The child's actual work at the chalkboard should also be patterned after the sequences of development of movement control. This statement has been repeated frequently in this book and bears repeating again, without apology, because of the importance of keeping all guidance in accord with the expected trend and flow of the child through the time-growth-maturation-learning sequence.

You will note that the diagrams show a large size chalk (see Figure 21). This is emphatically recommended because there is no possibility the child can hold it with the same white-knuckled fisted grip so common in the use of a pencil. The best chalk is called "railroad chalk" and is very large in diameter. It is usually yellow in a shade that has been scientifically determined as the most visible

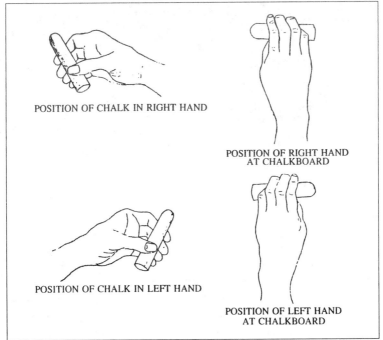

POSITION OF CHALK IN RIGHT HAND

POSITION OF RIGHT HAND
AT CHALKBOARD

POSITION OF CHALK IN LEFT HAND

POSITION OF LEFT HAND
AT CHALKBOARD

Figure 21. Holding the chalk.

color on the green chalkboard. It can be obtained from major crayon companies or large school supply sources. If this large chalk cannot be found, there is a triple sized chalk which is much better than the usually available chalk that can be found in almost every supermarket. Make an effort to find this best chalk. It will assist your child in all of the chalkboard activities being recommended here as beneficial to classroom progress.

There is a best way to hold the chalk and this is a preliminary to how the child will also hold a pencil. First of all, the chalk should be wrapped with masking tape so it can be more firmly gripped by the child's fingertips. This wrapping also keeps it from shattering if it is dropped upon a hard floor. The manner in which chalk should be held is illustrated in Figure 21, and your child is now ready for the basic routines which will help him find the arm, hand and finger combinations preparatory to all the crayon and pencil tasks of the classroom.

1. Bi-Manual Circles

The child who demonstrates any degree of spasticity (which is usually present to some degree in every child having difficulty in school) should work on circular movements first, using both hands in unison (See Figure 22A.). These can be varied through the developmental directions also:

   a. Right hand moving clockwise while left moves counterclockwise

   b. Left moves clockwise and right moves in the counter direction

   c. Both moving clockwise

   d. Both moving counterclockwise

The use of both hands at the same time in this activity is worthy of further discussion. This is in no manner intended to influence "dominancy" or "preference" of a hand, but to get all possible control of each hand and to emphasize each in the bilateral relationships. "Hand preference" in cultural activity comes as the child develops hand skills and will only result from dexterity of movement. Some children have not established "dominancy" because

Figure 22A. The rhythm and coordination of both hands in the movements of making circles on the chalkboard will be reinforced by the visual judgments of the size and shapes of the circles being produced.

they have not achieved enough dexterity in either hand to determine which hand will be "dominant." Use and development of both hands in basic guidance routines is a prerequisite for any of the more discrete or distinct skills which lead to writing and refined manipulative actions.

2. Bi-Manual Straight Lines

The child holds a piece of chalk in each hand and moves both hands at the same time in various patterns of movement as in Figure 22-B.

Figure 22B. A child cannot fully perceive a straight line unless he can also draw a straight line. Bilaterally drawn lines on the chalkboard provide the opportunity to "feel and see" lines like those he will be drawing in his primary workbooks.

Bi-manual chalk lines are made by the child to connect A1 and A2 with the "bull's-eye"; then B1, B2 and the center spot, etc. A1 and A2 should be placed far enough apart on the board so your child can reach them with full arm extension while standing approximately 12 or 14 inches in front of the board. All other outside dots are placed to complete a spoke pattern, which requires the same arm extension by your child. The movements of hands are from outside dots to central spot, and back again from the bull's-eye to dots in all possible variations of direction. There is a development sequence here also, which should be followed.

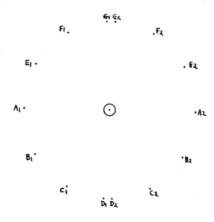

Figure 23. This illustrates the dot to center point pattern for practice in bilateral control of hands when drawing straight lines.

A. All hand movements in the horizontal directions:

    a. The right hand draws a chalk line from A2 to the center, and left hand draws from A1 to center. Thus, hands are both moving at the same time from outside dots to center dot. (See Figure 23 for dot pattern.)

    b. Both chalks are placed on the center dot. The right hand draws a chalk line from center to A2 while left draws from center to A1. Again hands are to be kept in bilateral movement.

    c. The right hand draws a chalk line from the center to A2 while left hand is drawing from A1 to center.

d. Have your child reverse the directions of his hand movements so the right draws from A2 to center, and left from center to A1.

B. Have your child use A dots, G dots and the center, as starting points and destination in the varieties described above. For example: right hand draws from G2 to center while the left hand draws from A1 to center, etc. This gives your child an opportunity to combine horizontal and vertical movements of arms while drawing the lines.

C. Have your child use combinations of the diagonally placed dots for all possible two-hand movements while drawing lines on the same chalkboard pattern.

D. Finally have your child make vertical and horizontal movements in every conceivable combination for practice on the same chalkboard pattern.

It is important that your child strive to keep all arm and hand movements coordinated so both hands reach their destination at the same time. This develops freedom of movement and kinesthetic (muscle feeling) awareness of arm and hand positions. When your child starts these routines, you may note that he turns head and eyes to watch and guide his chalk lines. As skill in movement is developed urge him to keep his visual attention on the center dot but to be aware of his hand movements "out of the corner of his eyes." This assists him to develop and widen his visual span for motion and orientation. This is an important but not commonly known factor in many activities. The superior athlete, the safe driver and the good hunter all have great need of this ability to be aware of what goes on around them, as well as inspecting the object at which they are looking.

3. Follow the Dots

These activity books for children are familiar to most parents. Frequent and lengthy search of children's book displays has not found many of these which are suitable for the young child. Either the child does not recognize numbers, or his concept of number sequence is inadequate. The ability to connect dots with a line demands the skill of visualizing the direction the line must take to get to the next dot. This skill is certainly not one that comes in a happenstance manner and is a perception which must be developed by the child.

The usual kindergarten workbooks do not contain enough of this activity. These workbooks usually demand that some sort of a line be drawn connecting two hats, two chairs, or a word with a picture of an object. Too frequently the teacher OKs the page if the two somethings are connected by a line, no matter how circuitous or crooked. This wandering line does not adequately develop the visualization and interpretations of directions. Here especially the parents can assist their child by a simplified follow-the-dot exercise.

A dot is placed on the chalkboard by the parent and the child is instructed to place his chalk upon this dot. The adult then places another dot on the board in any position and the child is instructed to connect the dots with a line. He is now instructed to hold his chalk on the second dot so he will be ready to move immediately to the third dot, which will next be put on the board. This can continue until the board is full of dots with lines in every conceivable direction. Of course it is important to urge quick full arm movements, which produce straight lines between the dots. Children enjoy this routine because it can provide a situation which develops anticipation, visualization and speed, fluidity and skill of movement.

With another bit of ingenuity the parent can so place the dots that the finished sequence of lines will represent simple outlines of actual things. All young children are tremendously pleased when they view the results and find that they have drawn a picture! First grade children can count the dots aloud as they connect them, thus obtaining further experience in the sequence of numbers. Second grade and even some first grade children can number each new dot before they connect it to utilize and apply the number-sequence concepts they are learning in school. Only now will they be ready for the multiple number dot books from the local stores.

The child can now enjoy the satisfaction of free-hand drawing and spontaneous designs that he can put on the chalkboard. He has gained the primary skills of movement and direction as applied to one of the tools of writing. The routines, as given here, are the "creeping-stones" to drawing and penmanship. If all parents could observe the pencil, or crayon, and paper productions of a child before and after these routines, they would be fully convinced of the value of a chalkboard to the child, and no playroom would ever be without it.[22]

You will have noted that all of the routines described in this section are closely related to classroom activities, or the readiness for these academic tasks. Eye-hand movements (and all other movement patterns) just for the sake of movement are not enough. All movement skills should have the very real and important goal of greater success in the classroom. This is the 12- to 17-year "occupation" of most children, and all of the activities in this book have this goal as the underlying purpose and reason.

C—EYE MOVEMENT PATTERNS
(Procedures for the development of visual inspection skills)

How well a child sees the world and the objects and tasks therein is determined by how well the visual inspection abilities have been developed. This all starts in early infancy when the child visually locates and inspects all those things found in the immediately surrounding space. The discrete control of eye movements is essential if visual discriminations are to become effective and efficient. The child who lacks these eye movement controls cannot "see at a glance" and must spend additional time and effort in making visual judgments and visual decisions. Any inadequacy here, which allows jerky or restricted eye movements, will deter all visual interpretations. Reams of clinical and laboratory reports now show that if the two eyes do not synchronize or move quickly and accurately, school achievement is usually low--or even lacking. Standard tests, such as the Primary Mental Abilities Test, show significant relationships between eye movement skills and the test sections: Visual Matching, Copying, and Space.

Classroom studies by teachers especially interested in children "who were smart in everything except schoolwork" showed that ocular motilities were one significant key to school achievement. One group of children who were given eye movement practice as a part of the schoolroom program gained from nine to 13 academic months in three calendar months. These eye movement routines are now a standard procedure in several other classrooms in this and neighboring school systems and the statistical analysis of the results has been published as a doctoral thesis (Dorothy Simpson, Ph.D., "Perceptual Readiness and Beginning Reading." Purdue University, Lafayette, Indiana). This report shows beyond any doubt that children who enter school with skillful and coordinated ocular movement abilities immediately get off to a good start in academic routines.

There have been literally hundreds of studies of vision and school performance, but only in the past few years has any research been directed to ocular motilities. Most studies have considered visual acuity (clarity of sight) and its relationship to academic performance. Of course there was little or no correlation found in these studies because visual acuity at a distance of 20 feet (the standard wall chart position) and reading from a book at 13 to 16 inches are not comparable activities. Eye movements and reading are much more closely related activities so the later research has been productive and informative.[36,50,51,56,29,69,74,70,45,46,48,75,30,57,38,39]

As stated above, the child who enters school with eye movement skills has a tremendous advantage. Considerate parents can do much to assure this advantage for their children to gain these ocular readinesses. Some of these routines can be done satisfactorily with very young children, and the first recommendations that follow are for these children or for the older child who has not gained adequate control of eye movements.

1. Sit in front of your child and have six or eight small toys in your lap and out of your child's sight. Pick up one of these toys (or interesting objects) with your right hand and hold it to your child's left side, urging him to look at it quickly and to name it before you take it away. While the child's attention is on this first object, pick up another with your left hand and hold it off to the child's right side. As soon as the first object has been identified, urge the inspection and naming of the second one. While your child is looking at this one, pick up another with your right hand and repeat the sequence. Keep this game going as long as you can with quick changes of the objects, urging your child to look back and forth from right to left as quickly as

possible, "moving ONLY your eyes." Avoid saying: "Do not move your head," but assist your child on how to move eyes without any head movement. The objects should be held slightly wider than the points of your child's shoulders so there is greater possibility of eye movements WITHOUT head movements. As you can observe quick and accurate eye movements without head movement, hold the objects in random positions so your child will have to move eyes into all directions and positions of gaze. The best targets for this routine are the little toys you can obtain in any variety store. These need not be elaborate, but they should also be used only for this activity and put away between practice sessions. Thus, your child will not play with them so frequently that interest and novelty are lost.

2. Make a practice of handing things to your child from the sides. When you butter a piece of bread for him, do not place it on the plate but hold it to one side so it must be LOOKED FOR and REACHED FOR. Do this in every possible situation to avoid those positions of visual attention that are only directly in front of your child.

3. Urge your child to look at you when you speak to him. When you wish to express a request or give an instruction, say, "Look at me, please," and then make your comment. Every time this is done, your child will get the practice of looking and listening, the basis for all the EYE CONTACT that is so important to communication and the interpersonal relationships in the classroom.

4. When your child asks for something, urge him to point to it as well as naming it. When your child makes a request of you, say, "Show me, please," or "Point to it, please," so there is the practice in the combinations of looking, pointing and speaking. This will help to prepare him for reading aloud in the classroom.

5. Attach a string to a ball that is about three inches in diameter so it can be hung from a light fixture, a doorway, or a ceiling hook).

    A. Have this ball at your child's nose level when he is facing it. Swing it gently from side to side, and to and from him, with instructions to watch it carefully as it swings.

    B. Variety holds the child's interest and allows identification practice when the stick-ons are verbalized by your child. Hang the ball about three feet above the floor. Have your child lie supine directly under the ball. Swing it in a rather large circle and instruct your child to watch it carefully until it comes almost to a stop.

When your child's eyes move smoothly in both A and B, stick small letters and numbers on the ball to require more discriminating visual attention. Assure this by asking your child to call out the letters or numbers being located.

Figure 24. The tracking movements induced by the swinging ball are the practicings for the movements of eyes across a line of print in a textbook. Small letters, numbers, pictures, and even words can be stuck onto the ball for variety of targets. This variety holds the child's interest and allows identification practice when the stick-ons are verbalized by your child.

6. Simpson found that children enjoyed helping each other in developing these special eye movement abilities. She attached a small toy airplane to the eraser of a pencil with a pin. One child would hold the pencil and "make the airplane fly" in front of another child's face. The second child would be the "plane spotter" and would have to keep eyes on the plane at all times through all of its movements. If at this time, the "pilot" caught the "spotter" losing visual contact, a point was scored for him. Then the two children would change positions and the game would start again.

This is an excellent procedure because it brings motivations while each child is gaining visual awarenesses and the eye movement skills without realizing they are working at it. This and other routines bring practice in the eye movements which are similar to those needed for reading activities. When eyes follow these moving targets, the ocular actions are those needed for visual scan and search. As the child looks for the objects being shown, there is practice in those same movements required in scanning a page for a particular word or phrase.

7. Have your child hold right and left forefingers erect, about 10 inches in front of eyes. Urge your child to look quickly from left finger to right finger, continuing back and forth several times. Urge speed of eyes and accuracy of "landings" on finger tips. The goal is to achieve rhythm, speed and fluidity of the "jump" between fingers, with immediate "landings" of both eyes. This activity is related to those eye movements in leaving the end of a line of print and quickly finding the beginning of the next line.

Some children have considerable difficulty developing the rhythmic movements here. If this is true with your child, pace the action by touching each finger in time with your counting, or with music. A young child's attention can be held if you will use a very small toy animal and ask him to "watch the bunny hop from finger to finger."

8. Have your child hold a pencil erect about 6 inches in front of his nose. Request your child to look from the pencil to numbers on a calendar on the wall across the room, and to do this as quickly and accurately as possible. Then, back to pencil, to calendar numbers, repeating for 12 or 15 round trips. Be sure both targets are being seen clearly, quickly and singly. As this becomes easier, have your child move the pencil closer to the face, and repeat the 12 or 15 round trips.

This routine gives practice in two special movement patterns which will be very helpful to your child in the classroom. It improves the ability to shift eyes quickly from the words on the chalkboard to the lines on the worksheet on the desk, or from the textbook to the teacher's face and back to the book. It also improves the speed of visual focusing, and the discriminations at all of the various distances involved in classroom activities.

Another word of caution and advice is necessary here. Most

children will show improvements after six or eight sessions of practice in these routines. If a child cannot accomplish the eye movement patterns and the more specific ocular movements required in the above activities, a complete optometric evaluation of visual development should be immediately arranged. The optometric profession has developed and standardized observation and examination sequences which give reliable appraisals of children as young as 3, and in many instances, as young as 12 months. Parents sometimes make the mistake of waiting until a child is older, hoping the problem will be outgrown or just go away. Any visual problem existing actually gets worse with time because the visual system, and its information, is so important to total development that a child will frequently make undesirable adaptations to avoid confusions. Some of these adaptations result in a "lazy eye" that is much more difficult to recover at later ages. Likewise, this early vision care can prevent eye movement problems or eye team problems that could contribute to academic problems an alert child should not be having. An ounce of early preventive care if worth more than a pound of very difficult attention later.

D—VISION--LANGUAGE PATTERNS
(Procedures for the development of communication skills)

The intricacies and subtleties of language in the human have received broad attention in the past few years. There is now a greater interdisciplinary interest than ever before because of the realizations that language development demands the contributions of all the actions systems and all of the information processing systems in the human. Further, the development of communication skills depends upon all of the interpretation abilities of both the sender and the receiver of the messages. For example, body language has only been fully explored by researchers and students of human behavior in the past two or three decades, and this mode of human communication is extremely dependent upon the visual discriminations of the interpreter. If the receiver is to visually interpret the body language of another person he must have a kinesthetic empathy for the messages being expressed in the body language of another person. In addition to visual and kinesthetic awarenesses, the receiver must make judgments of the relevances between the tone of the sender's voice and the emphasis of the facial expressions and/or gestures being used. If a mother's face shows definite disapproval but her voice is soft, gentle and forgiving, the true message may be missed by the child. Likewise, if the body language shows tensions and disagreement, the words being used may be a complete contradiction and the receiver will have great difficulty knowing what his response should be. One's actions frequently do speak louder than words. Language, another of God's masterpieces given to man, is made up of much more than mere speech, and parents need to know all the avenues there are for its development in their children.[36,20,5,18,29,67,68,58,42]

Language Is a Visual Activity

Language extends from the cooing of the infant and the lullaby of the mother to the abstract and almost alien verbalizations of the expert in the language of the electronic space age. Generally, the very young child's language development places the primary demands upon speech and hearing. While the child is learning to control the muscles of mouth, lips, tongue, throat and diaphragm for speech noises, he depends to a very great extent upon his audition to check the accuracy of his own words and to be sure these match the words used by others. There is no doubt but that the child learns his mother tongue by imitation and the results he achieves from the appropriate use of the words so learned. This imitative language serves the child very well as long as he remains in the environment in which little mispronunciations, or slurred phrases, are understood so the "baby talk" is ignored by siblings and parents. When this child walks into the classroom there are immediate requirements for more accurate communications and comprehensions, and the child finds that his basic speech and hearing abilities are not quite enough for this new situation.[20]

Suddenly there is the discovery of the need for the more critical visual discriminations of the other speaker's mouth shapes and facial expressions, and the learner must bring new visual ability into this process of communication. Here the child finds there are facial expressions and gestures available to him for expanded communication with others. Often this is the child's most vivid experience with those actions which frequently do speak louder than words and that these actions are the signals which must be seen as well as being heard. Here a relationship is being established between many special movement patterns and vision, and these will become a major factor in the ability to read. A little boy is supposed to have said, "Shucks, readin' is jist talkin' wrote down." This is not quite all of the story. If talkin' can be wrote down, it also means that what is written for visual inspections and deciphering must also become talkin' for the completions of the communications expected out of all of this. Further, if talkin' is to be wrote down, there must be opportunities for the hand to feel all that the eyes are seeing. As visual tactual integrations are achieved, there comes the ability to "see" what a number, letter or word "feels" like, and to "feel" what each of these symbols "looks" like. The contributions which come out of the ability to write bring language development to broader levels of communication than speech alone can possibly furnish. Much more detailed discussion of the visual tactual combinations so important to classroom tasks will come in the next few pages. At this point, emphasis must be given to the visual symbols as communication components that match speech in the language complex in the human.[44,52,56,29,70,76,68,48,53]

It is not long before the child discovers that the books thrust into his hands contain many perplexing confusions. There are too many words there which do not contain the visual and speech- auditory matches upon which he has come to depend. English is phonetically erratic, and unless new language skills are quickly achieved, there are many printed or written words which may never be fully mastered. It only requires one example to illustrate this problem the child faces. Look at the word *slough*. How should it be pronounced? Should it sound like *through*, or *enough*, or like a*lthough*? When this word, and many others like it, appears in isolation there is neither visual nor auditory clue to its most likely pronunciation. If it is to be correctly pronounced and used, it must be either seen or heard, in full written or spoken context. When the whole sentence containing this word is neither audible nor visible, it becomes one of those words which cause difficulties for many individuals at any age. This is also an illustration why neither a total phonics nor a total visual approach to printed words in the primary readers will suffice for children in the throes of learning to read. There must be an approach which fully incorporates the speech-hearing combinations with the sight-speech combinations, and all the contradictions which may exist, or the learner will not find these integrations which are so essential to success in a world now pivoting upon symbols. A "return to phonics" without a concomitant "return to sight vocabulary" is not sufficient for the mastery every child is expected to achieve in the art of reading.

There is still another aspect to these elaborate interchanges and interweavings of the systems involved in language development where the visual auditory relationships are significant. A 12-year-old boy enrolled in a special school provided insights to his complex which will bear detailing here. Bob was a splendid word caller after extensive training in the phonetic approach, and could read aloud from almost any book handed to him. When asked what the story was all about, Bob replied, "I don't know--I was not listening." When we determined that Bob was not just testing the authority of his teacher, a carefully designed playback equipment was set up so Bob would be more aware of his voice, without amplification. Thus, we judged it would be more likely Bob would listen to what he was reading aloud. He had only read for a few moments when he stopped in midsentence with a surprised look on his face. When asked why he had stopped, Bob replied, "I just found out what a comma sounds like." Bob brought the emphatic realization that these little black marks on paper are representations having very specific clues on what is to be heard as well as seen. In the case of the comma, Bob discovered it to be a bit of silence, a pause in vocalizing. Here was the discovery of the ability to go beyond some memorized rules of grammar to know what a punctuation mark will sound like from the looks of it, and to know what marks should be visible on paper from the sounds of a voice. It was most interesting that from this time on Bob read with more attention to punctuation and with more expressiveness, and with a definite rise in reading comprehension.

Vision and Audition Are a Team

The behavioral optometrist is tangentially very interested in audition because of its many similarities to vision, and because of the role audition plays in visual spatial orientations. The auditory specialist knows it is the information the listener achieves out of what he hears that is more significant than the results of hearing acuity tests. Thus, these clinicians differentiate between hearing and audition just as the optometrist differentiates between sight and vision. Both informed audiologists and behavioral optometrists recognize that audition and vision are the human's long distance receptors. All the other information receiving systems depend upon nearby stimuli. Taction is only as good as the length of an arm. Olfaction is only as good as the atmosphere that brings odors to the nose. Gustation is only as good as the length of the tongue. Proprioception is only as good as the internal signals from muscles and joints. In high contrast, vision and audition can reach across space as extensions of all the other information systems through personal experiences and all of the language signals. Children depend upon their combinations of vision and audition for the first interpretations of spatial distances and spatial positions. When they see a parent at a distance and find the auditory signals are not the same as they are when being held by a parent, they begin to develop a primitive concept of intervening distances. When they see themselves in a mirror and suddenly realize they cannot touch "that baby" who seems to be talking to them, they find a contradiction that brings temporary confusions between the visual and the auditory signals. As these confusions are cleared, new appreciations of visual space and auditory space are achieved and both systems have been critically essential to the clarifications.

The wealth of opportunities for language development in early childhood brings experiences which are foundations for academic readiness. All that is included in the development of "perceptual skills" reduces to the learned ability to discriminate JNDs (Just Noticeable Differences). Children probably begin interpretive processes by making comparisons and categorizations. The infant expresses comfort and security while surrounded by family, those individuals the infant has put into a consistent category as being those who are seen, heard and felt most often and most reliably. First JNDs may be made between family and strangers, and when these are achieved by the infant, discomfort with the differences is often expressed. The infant's visual world has been described as a "big, blazing, buzzing confusion" because of all the JNDs there are surrounding the infant. It is more likely this environment is not the jumble of confusion for the infant we adults think it to be because the baby is already making discriminations and organizations of those JNDs important to him. In this very complex and constantly evolving process, the infant finds the vision-language patterns to be the components upon which much reliance can be placed. The visual tactual information is most available during all waking moments and next the visual auditory information comes out of every contact with members of the family. Eventually, the infant's own attempts to vocalize his needs and responses bring the information that solidifies all of the other bits of information being achieved. As the infant's own language skills develop through use and practice, there is the preparation for the day when the move to the printed word, those abstractions for all the experiences up until now, truly becomes "jist talkin' wrote down."[12]

Children Need to Talk to Themselves

Since "good talkin'" makes definite contributions to "good readin'" the more extensive and accurate the vocabulary, the more available the child will be to the primary reading teacher. It is also well established that a child's vocabulary is established and enhanced by primary experiences. Numerous authorities on child development state that the child's first language is "action language"--all those words that express the child's own actions. This is very reasonable since the child's own movements and the results of these movements should be the easiest to talk about. One authority states it thus: "The early language of the child is not communicative at all but is his own naming language. Its purpose is to attach a label which 'packages' the developing perception so it can be held where it is in order that the child may then go on to learn something else. He can come back to the 'package' and, by use of the label he has assigned to it, integrate the first perception with another for the formation of a new concept. Frequently, the young child is not interested in talking to anybody--he is talking to hear himself talk and to practice those labels he has already put upon things he has seen or experienced." This talking the child does to himself can be encouraged and utilized in many ways to give the child broader understanding of the words he is practicing, as well as just enjoying the conversations with himself. Behavioral optometrists have frequently found their vision therapy to be much more effective when their patients talk about what they are doing as they do it. This is the extension and application of the internal language all humans rely upon for the phrasing and meanings they wish to use in conversation.[4,20]

We must emphasize that a lack of development in articulation could be the result of a hearing problem. If hearing tests turn out to be normal, there might still be an audition problem. Audition, like vision, is the *learned* ability to interpret what is heard. Subtle likenesses and differences exist in sounds that can be heard just as these JNDs exist in shapes that can be seen. The child who lacks skills in these auditory discriminations will have trouble remembering what he heard and he may not be able to fully interpret an experience because its sounds were not amply discerned. These children often fail to remember stories read to them because of the incompletions or inaccuracies of the auditory inputs. They confuse words that sound alike and they forget when sent on errands. Or they may return with the wrong object because of this auditory confusion. These children are too often accused of not paying attention to what they were told, and they often hear an adult saying, "Why didn't you listen to me?" These children may also have more than the usual difficulty with phonics because of the many similarities in this sort of program.

If there is any question about the child's hearing acuity, it must be thoroughly appraised as early as possible. However, again there is a close resemblance to visual problems. Training and guidance can do much to overcome the problems which may exist, especially after a hearing problem is eliminated. Alert speech and hearing therapists know that a child can profit from auditory training as much, or more, than he may profit from mere speech training.

The following procedures will not attempt to suggest methods for hearing and speech practice. Speech and hearing therapy is not the prerogatives of this book. Its real purpose lies in the vision language relationships that can evolve out of seeing, listening, visualizing, saying and doing for the extension of skill in communication abilities. In general, the activities of children in the first five to seven years follow the sequence of do and say, see and name, hear and imitate, listen and repeat, inspect and tell and visualize and describe. Thus, most of the components of language and vision are incorporated to the child's benefit.

1. Make a game for verbs--walk, run, hop, work, play, etc. Question your child about what a boy can do, a girl, a mother, a father, a dog, a truck, a tractor, etc.

2. Encourage your child to talk about his interests and activities.

3. Make a game for adverbs. Walk quickly, slowly, sadly, quietly, noisily, happily, etc.

4. Make a game for prepositions. Have him put an object in, on, under, beside, below, above, behind the box.

5. Make a game for adjectives. Have him bring you something blue, red, big, little, striped, smooth, hard, soft, fuzzy, etc. Have him pretend he is big, brave, happy, unhappy, kind, old, young, etc. Have him describe objects on the dinner table, his parents, his clothes, your clothes, etc. Here once more we find the

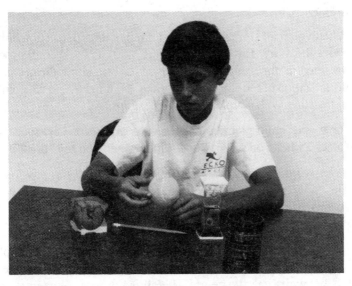

Figure 25. The vision language relationships which produce the abilities for oral reading originate in the identification and description of familiar objects. This "see and say" activity can become a speed game that parents can use to assist the child in his integrations of vision, taction and language.

importance of visual judgments and discriminations as a part of activity.

6. Have him name and classify objects and activities. Have him name all the fruits he can, then all the vegetables he can, then furniture, animals, cars, toys and colors. Have him talk about Mother's activities, Father's activities, and his own activities. His skill in visualization will determine the number of objects and activities he can classify, and he will be building the associations between visualizations, articulation and language in this procedure.

7. Show your child an interesting picture. Let him hold and handle it first. Encourage him to talk about the picture after his visual inspection of it. Help him to increase the length of his sentences which describe the picture.

8. Encourage your child to imitate the sounds of an airplane, train, auto, clock, animals, etc. The ability to imitate these sounds gives him control of the lips, mouth, tongue and throat positions for good speech.

9. When you read stories to your child remember to question him about the story. Have him retell the story. If he becomes too involved in unnecessary details, or if his retelling indicates his visualization of the story is inaccurate, get him back to the point of the story with simple, leading questions.

10. Have your child give the opposites to words you say, such as "black" when you say "white," "little" when you say "big," etc.

11. Say a word as slowly as possible, then as quickly as possible. The slow performance will prepare the child for blending sounds in phonetics later in school. The slow and then fast performance will aid in flexibility and control of articulation.

12. Play games or hold conversations requiring different types of voices--a baby with a tiny voice, a mother with a medium voice, a father with a deep voice, etc. This allows the use of imaginative visualization in relation to the child's own family. The mannerisms of others as seen by a child will be related in his "acting" just as the speech tones will be reflected by his voice.

13. Give your child a chance to "rattle on" once in awhile. Some children do not need to be given this opportunity while others are "shushed" too frequently. Speech skill comes from practice just as all other abilities are developed by practice.

14. Tell simple stories of three or four sentences about your child's everyday activities. Have him retell it to you as accurately as possible. Keep these stories related to his own activities so visualizations can assist him in the retelling.

15. Tap on the table several times. Your child is instructed to listen, count mentally, and then tell the number of your taps. If he has difficulty, tap on his hand or knee so he feels the taps as he counts. When using a hard surface, vary by tapping loudly, softly, slowly, quickly, and then in irregular rhythm.

16. Have your young child listen to jingles and nursery rhymes, especially those which contain similar sounds such as Baa Baa Black Sheep, Bye Baby Bunting, Hickory Dickory Dock, etc. Repeating in unison is helpful, as well as choral speaking of rhymes, sentences, or even single difficult words.

17. Urge your child to identify noises and locate them whenever possible. Again, visual localization integrates and reinforces the auditory experiences. This also gives him the opportunity to check his auditory judgment against his visual impression.

18. Whenever possible in conversation have your child watch your lips and mouth. Thus, what he sees and what he hears will fit together so he can utilize both vision and audition in conversation. We adults unconsciously depend upon seeing the other person's mouth movements and facial expressions to get the most meaning from what is being said to us. Your child should also have the same opportunity to learn the use of these visual reinforcements to the auditory skills. Words that sound alike may not "look" alike, and thus a child is given further help in auditory discriminations by seeing the variation in lip and mouth shapes while you are saying these words.

19. Have your child listen to words beginning with the same sounds. Have him suggest other words which begin with the same sounds. Speak a number of words beginning with the same

sound and then add one beginning with a different sound, such as: horse, house, hen, hurry, car. Have your child repeat the different word.

20. Encourage your child to repeat or sing the jingles he hears on radio or television.

21. There is a great variety of audio tapes having books that duplicate in words and pictures all the child will hear on the tape. These must be very carefully explored to be sure those you obtain contain stories of greatest interest to your child. One of these, just appraised, supposedly helps a child to learn the ABCs, but the words are very poorly selected and will not appeal to many children needing to learn the alphabet. Too frequently these tapes and the accompanying books are designed by adults who think they know what is of interest to children. You should not purchase any of these unless you can get into the plastic package and explore the material to be confident it is appropriate for your child. When choosing these materials be very certain the words your child will hear and see are already in his vocabulary. Do not expect these tapes and books to lead your child into new words. Introduce these in your everyday conversations and in situations that will be a meaningful experience for your child. An early 1940s authority on children's reading skills made a comment that is more appropriate today. "We must constantly remember that a child gets no meaning FROM a printed word, but must at all times bring meaning TO the printed word."

Parents can make the audio tapes to fit their child's favorite books. In fact, this is the way to assure the child's interest, and almost every child has several books he wants read over and over to him at bedtime. Simply turn on the tape recorder and read the book your child likes. Do just as the commercial packagers do and ring a bell, or tap on a drinking glass, each time the page is to be turned. Such programming of the books which best hold your child's interest allows him to hold the book, and will be a splendid substitute should there be an evening when pressures prevent your reading to him.

Start Reading to Your Infant

There cannot be too much emphasis put upon the importance of reading to your children. Children who have been read to regularly are the children who find the joys of reading through this vision language experience. There is ample evidence that those children who are the spontaneous readers, who learn to read all by themselves before going to school, were read to by parents almost from the moment of birth. It is now obvious the more a child is read to in the first five years, the more likely he is to be a good reader by the time he is thrust into reading in the classroom. Reading to your children on a routine daily basis can assure you of their success in mastery of the printed words academia insists they know as quickly as possible in the primary grades.

22. Have your child close his eyes while a member of the family speaks. Have him identify the voice and where the speaker is located in the room by pointing with eyes still closed. By combining the pointing with the identification your child will make a visual localization as well as an auditory localization. This assists the integration in the mechanisms of seeing and hearing.

23. Give your child oral directions involving two activities, then three, four or more as he can accomplish them. For example: "Pick up the magazine, put it on the table, and sit on the chair." Repeat until your child can do it just as you said it. If difficulty is encountered, repeat each direction as he does it until he can do them following your directions. State each direction slowly so your child can visualize the action he is to take in following the instruction. This activity develops auditory span, and when the child has learned to hear it completely and comprehensively the first time it is stated, it can save parents and teachers much time and repetition. Thus, as he grows and learns to depend upon his auditory discriminations, his judgments and decisions will be speeded.

E—VISUALIZATION PATTERNS

(Procedures for the development of interpretation skills)

The spiral of development and your child's acquisition of the skills described in the previous sections should now have brought him to that level of performance where vision alone can provide him with much information about the world and its contents. It should no longer be necessary for him to use his hands to touch, lift or measure the familiar objects he sees. It is now essential that procedures be provided which will assist him in learning that his vision can give him dependable information regarding size, texture, approximate weight, shape, distance, etc. Only thus will his hands be completely free to serve him as the tools of productivity.

Toys furnish experiences of visual comparisons--the visual relationships in size, shape and solidity. When your child has learned to make these simple comparisons, it will be possible for him to visually discriminate more elaborate relationships. Frequently space intervenes and does not permit a child to utilize hands for tactual information; therefore, he must make his decisions and judgments via vision alone. Again vision alone must give him the necessary information and skill should be acquired in the activities which will eventually assist him to see and recognize the differences and similarities between B and D, b and d, H and N, p and q, and many other letter forms. Inadequacies within this phase of visual development permit the reversals in spelling and writing which plague so many primary grade children. Rote training alone does not solve the reversal problem. With proper preparation, as outlined in this book, the child's own skill in recognition of details and his ability to see that "B is like a D, but B is different from a D because it has a little line in the middle," helps to solve the reversal, or substitution problems.

Practice and training in making visual comparisons is of importance, and the alert parent can provide many opportunities for a child to exercise and develop this skill. This skill revolves around vision and use of the visual mechanism, and here is another example of learning to see. Acuity of 20/20 alone does not assure that your child is capable of making accurate interpretative discriminations of the details that count.

There are at least three components of visual interpretation skills that will be given the most consideration in the following procedures. These are: a. visual comparison skill, b. visual memory skill, and c. visual projection skill. These are also given here in the development sequence that will most likely assure successful participation by the child. It should be noted once more that these components do not occur as separate entities in children's performance but are separate here for convenience in description and for emphasis upon the activity requested of the child.

Parents can assist their child in making visual discriminations with the following procedures:

1. Have your child put together simple jigsaw puzzles.

Research shows a high correlation between jigsaw puzzles and reading ability. After a child has learned the shape and form of letters, he uses shape and form of words as one cue to their identity. The relationships between the shape of a puzzle piece and the shape of a word are easy to understand when one stops to give it consideration.

Not Every Puzzle is Educational

A WORD OF WARNING! Many puzzles can be more confusing than helpful. Pieces can be so intricate, or so very much alike, that a fully completed puzzle cannot be achieved by a child. Some puzzles have color splashes or color blends that

Figure 26. Properly chosen jigsaw puzzles can be a rainy day pastime that will assist your child in recognizing and matching shapes and contours. Good puzzles also provide practice in the recognition of the JNDs found in many of the pieces. An extremely complex puzzle may so irritate a child that a dislike of puzzles might prevent his gaining this important pre-symbol experience.

create confusion. Others cut animals up into the shape of objects, or even airplanes, and a child is bewildered over which cues to follow. Parents should choose very carefully when obtaining puzzles for children, and they should attempt to see the puzzle *as a child sees it* when confronted with the task of assembly.

2. Have your child match and compare objects in the kitchen cupboards. Sorting dishes and silverware is a basic visual comparison activity. Canned goods can be stacked according to label. Colors, numbers, words, etc. on cereal boxes can be used for visual comparison.

3. Use furniture, pictures, magazines, books and every other household object for your child's visual comparisons. Ask him how two chairs are alike, and how they are different. Ask him to describe the likenesses and differences in size, shape, weight, texture in all of the items that can be seen in any room. If he makes gross or unreasonable errors, urge him to check his visual judgments by touching or lifting the objects in question.

It was stated above that most children should now be ready to depend upon vision alone for reliable information. This does not mean that a child should not be allowed to return to tactual exploration to verify or correct his visual judgments. We adults do this frequently. If you will watch others in supermarkets, you will see frequent demonstrations of this return to hand contact "just to be sure the object is what it seems to be." A child in a variety store causes his mother, and perhaps the proprietor, much concern because he needs to verify his visual comparisons of the toy soldiers, or the toy cars, by getting his hands into the little bins that hold these toys. Although this need for verification may be restricted at the store, it should not be outlawed at home.

4. Have your child keep his eyes closed while you hand him some toy or familiar object. While keeping his eyes closed, he feels and explores the object with his fingers until he can tell you what it is. Some children cannot keep eyes closed. If your child is one of these, put the object into a paper sack so he can put his hand in and explore the object. He can now play "What Is It?" to gain visualization via the fingers and the tactual senses. The elaboration and transformation of an experience in texture to another

information system (vision and visualization) is valuable training and develops ability in touch, vision and speech skills through the processes by which the child identifies and describes what is felt without actually seeing it.

5. The words that occur in everyday table conversation can be most useful as preparation for the visual recognition of printed words. These food words are those receiving the reinforcement through the information systems of taste and smell, as well as by sight and touch. Here are more integrations for information systems so significant to the meaning of words. The grocery list will then provide the relevant experience of the symbols for all that was so pleasant (or perhaps not so pleasant) while eating. Now your child can bring meaning TO the curlicues on paper.

6. For variety in the "learning" trips to the market, tear off the labels from cans and small boxes. Have your child take these to the market and choose the replacements by matching the labels. Whenever possible in these two procedures say the name of the item as your child searches for it and finds it. A little extra time spent in the market adding this language reinforcement to his visual comparisons will be of real benefit to your child.

7. If you are one of the few Americans who walk to the market, use the many objects along the way for visual comparison practice. A single city block is unbelievably full of opportunities. We adults just need to remember that these are opportunities for training and guidance in the development of the visual skills your children need. The frequently traveled path to the market may be monotonously familiar to the adult, but it can be ever new and interesting to a child. His visual comparisons will help him learn to see all there is to see.

8. Be sure to make careful choices when obtaining coloring books for your child. The first ones you choose should have simple pictures with very heavy outlines. At first your child should not be especially encouraged to "stay inside the lines now." The difficulty he may have in coloring within the lines provides an opportunity for the visual comparison of where he did color and where he should have colored. His mistakes may discourage him if the pictures to be colored are too complex, but encouragement

and praise from you will assist him to do better, and his progress will be apparent as his visual comparison skills and hand dexterities develop.

It should be very obvious by now that these suggestions are leading your child into the eye-hand coordinations which are preparatory to the ability to write. Your child will make many discoveries when he enters the academic arena for the first time. He will be expected to learn to write by the end of his first year in school. The most elaborate and most complex of all the visual tactual combinations is the ability to write. When one stops to analyze what seems to be a very common act for a human, one quickly recognizes the visual aspects of the writing act, and the hand dexterities demanded here. Writing can be described as the visually guided, multidirectional movements of the hand. This complicated activity is expected to be so well mastered by each child that what he writes is legible enough and complete enough to communicate with others.

"My Name is Me"

Every child should be able to put his own name on paper BEFORE he goes to kindergarten. There is no law that says this ability must be taught by his first schoolroom teacher. Parents should check with the teacher a child will be having to find out how the letters should be made, and if other children with the same name are expected in the group. The child who recognizes and can write his own name will lose many less of his possessions upon which his mother has so carefully placed his name in the last weeks of August. Children are encouraged to draw simple pictures on their chalkboards. To the child his name is a "picture" of himself, and it is a very valued and personal "picture" because it "stands for me." Furthermore, as the child practices his name at the chalkboard, his comments, "That is not very good, is it?" or "I did it better this time," are evidences of the visual comparisons he is able to make.

The special movement patterns and the visual discriminations needed for writing have become such well established habits in the adult that parents do not fully realize how difficult it is for a youngster to master the writing process. A little exercise, here and now, will help parents to more fully understand what is being asked of a child when he is given a pencil and instructed to "make letters like those." Please follow these instructions:

Please *write* (do NOT print) your name in large letters in the air, using your preferred hand in the habitual writing fashion. Note how freely your hand and arm move, and how little thought you need to give to doing this. This ease comes from your having established a "motor pattern"--a habit pattern that requires no conscious attention. Now, *write* your name in the air again, this time using your other hand. You will note a very slight clumsiness, but you will have no difficulty completing your name because of the motor pattern you have achieved which allows this to still be a subconscious act. Now, *write* your name backwards using your non-preferred hand. Backwards, here, means you will start with the last letter in your name and write it from right to left. This presents a task for which you have not established a subconscious, habitual motor pattern, and you will find you have to give so much attention to the formation of each letter, and the directions of your arm and hand, that you may even lose the sequence of the letters, and suddenly you do not know how to spell the one word you have written more often than almost any other.

The child just learning to write finds himself in this same dilemma. He must give so much thought to all of the hand movements he frequently forgets what he is supposed to be writing. This confusion interferes with the acquisition of the motor patterns for each letter and the end result is confusion in visual tactual interpretations and the skills so critical to the tasks of the classroom. Further, this confusion interferes with the hoped for comprehension that writing is expected to generate.

And still another surprise! Now there is a new demand for remembering all the new things to be learned in the classroom, so this remembering will contribute to making the alphabet letters the teacher has across the top of the chalkboard in the front of the room. This memorizing has to be good for the "short term" and then good for the "long term." This means the child has to remember new letters for each lesson, and then over the weekend too. Now the importance of visualization becomes apparent since these memory abilities are the product of visualization abilities. This is especially true of long term memory ability where retention depends upon the individual's ability to bring up a mental image (a visualization) in the process of comparing what is being visually inspected with what has been previously seen. Although this is of extreme importance in the acquisition of a sight vocabulary, it is even more critical to spelling proficiency. As previously discussed, the phonetically silent letters and pronunciation confusions demand visualization skills. Lamentably, there are too many inherently intelligent children who are failing in spelling because they have not achieved this visualization ability. It is interesting to find how many adults are still poor spellers because of these same deficiencies in visualization.[43,77,78,33,34,79]

Clinical programs which incorporate practice in eye-hand coordinations and visualization have been productive at any age, with the greatest success coming before compensations become undesirable habits. The optometric therapy programs have been designed to use procedures already proven by other disciplines and adding what clinical practice has shown to be most effective. The integrations of the visual and tactual information systems have assisted children to find how to write letters of the alphabet so the motor patterns are achieved at the habit levels.[71,69,76]

There is an increasing discussion of the advantages and disadvantages of manuscript (print) writing and cursive (script) writing. One educators' journal devoted an entire section to this discussion and splendid points were made by proponents of each method for teaching the young child to write the English language (Academic Therapy, March, 1983). It is very interesting that the arguments swirled almost entirely around the tactual and kinesthetic aspects of the writing act. Only one presenter casually mentioned the role that visual discrimination skills play in the writing act. And visualization was not mentioned by any of the discussants.[68]

Where Are You Now, Mr. Palmer?

Many readers will remember the grade school hours spent in practicing the Palmer Method of cursive writing. Mr. Palmer wanted everyone to write beautifully, and his first lessons were: 1. how to hold the pencil with straight, relaxed fingers; 2. how to move the entire arm so the pencil hand would slide across the paper;

and 3. how to do circles, continuing ovals and push-pulls on paper with ruled lines that were widely spaced. Every day the writing lesson started with these circles, ovals and slightly tilted lines until there was an easy fluidity of arm and hand movements. This practice was a full preliminary to any approach to the letters of the alphabet. Mr. Palmer's cursive method, built on his desire for beautiful handwriting and legibility, brought results because it avoided the white-knuckled fist of today's child as he scribbles out each line of each letter in manuscript form. It also brought results in the spacing of letters and words on the page since the connections of letters in the words, and the spacing between words, came as a natural event in the total process. Further, there was one start and one stop to each word instead of many starts and stops on each letter in manuscript form. This closure of the letters into one "package"--the word--assists the learner to achieve the visual image of completion and contributes to the total form of the word which then becomes a visual clue that assists in word recognition. This closure into one unit also contributes to the kinesthetic impression that allows a child to set the motor pattern each word must have.

Reevaluations of how children learn to write have brought some desirable changes in writing lessons. In recent years, a method known as the D'Nealian program encourages children to add a stroke to each of the manuscript letters to assist in connecting the printed letters to each other. This is certainly a step in the right direction since it does help the child to use more arm and hand movement patterns.

Another forward step in behalf of children is a plastic sleeve that slips onto a pencil to guide fingers into a more relaxed posture. This prevents the white-knuckled fist so frequently observed in the classroom. It will probably be a replacement for the three-sided rubber sleeve being so widely used by primary children. This three-sided sleeve does help the child to keep the pencil from slipping and turning, but it does nothing to relieve the cramped, bent fingers almost every child demonstrates (see Figure 27).

The manuscript letter form is still widely favored because some-one offered the notion that a child would learn the alphabet more quickly and easily if the letters to be written were the same shapes

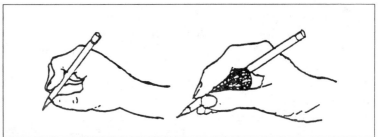

Figure 27. These two illustrations show the undesirable white- knuckled fist that creates so much stress and fatigue which become an interference to writing as a learning act, and the open hand that Mr. Palmer urged. The right illustration also show the sleeve that slips onto a pencil to prevent the bent fingers of the fisted grip, and the cramps which too frequently result.

as those he would see in his textbooks. This is not necessarily true. When a child really learns letters and words, it makes little difference in just what shape they are presented. Again, it is the knowledge the child brings TO the letters and words, and not the knowledge he is expected to get FROM them. If this were not true, we would not be able to read each other's writing--as bad as it has become for many individuals. When the child KNOWS letters and words, he will decipher them in almost any shape. This is especially true when he has the kinesthetic motor patterns and the visualizations with which to make these symbols.

Mr. McGuffey Revisited

Adults who are still insisting that the manuscript form should be maintained for the primary school child's writing lessons, regardless of the stress and fatigue it brings, should review the original McGuffey Readers. There they will find that Mr. McGuffey presented his very first lessons in both manuscript printing and cursive writing. He included both forms in the sentences on each page so there would be the visual experience with both. Mr. Palmer then came onto the scene and showed children how to obtain the most effective and efficient special motor patterns that would allow the interweaving of tactual skills with visual skills. If any adult observes a child who has laid the pencil down to flex and stretch a cramped hand and arm, he will see the evidence of the same stresses and confusions you experienced when you were asked to write your name backward with your non-preferred hand.

One more point in favor of cursive writing must be made. Every child who has not had the opportunity to achieve directionality skills and the special movement patterns discussed in this book will go through a period of "reversals" of letters and numbers. The reversal problems are much more common on manuscript letters, and appear most frequently on the letters "b" and "d," "p" and "q." Just looking at these letters here provides the clue for this reversal problem. Each of these letters has the same geometric form--a stick and a ball. The learner has to have the visual inspection skills which allow him to discriminate exactly where the ball is to be attached to the stick. Take a moment to write these same letters in cursive form and you will note that each of them has its own distinctive pattern; each requires a distinctive direction of hand movement. The JNDs here are much more evident than those in the ball and stick letters.

Again, there is no wish to encroach upon the prerogatives of the classroom teacher. Neither is there the intent that parents should teach handwriting as such. It continues to be the goal of this entire discussion of intellectual development that every child have the basic movement skills and the visual discrimination skills, which then allow the teacher to more effectively apply what she, or he, is so well trained to present in the academic environment. These visual and tactual skills can be achieved by almost every child *before* being thrust into the symbolic complexities of the classroom. Practice on the letters of the alphabet is practice on the elaborate shapes needed for every performance in the classroom. This valuable practice is best experienced at home on the big chalkboard you have obtained for your child.

In spite of the possibility that your child's teacher feels all in-classroom attention must be given to manuscript writing, hopefully there will be no resentment over the exploration of cursive writing at home. After all, the more ways one can do any one thing, the greater is the knowledge gained. And there are more similarities in most manuscript letters and the cursive letters than there are differences. The letters "s," "z," "r" and "l" in manuscript form are the only vivid dissimilarities.

Therefore, from a completely clinical, physiological and developmental viewpoint, the cursive forms for all letters will be recommended here as the homework for your child to achieve the eye-hand coordinations and the visual tactual reciprocities he needs for greater classroom readiness. Please note the sequence of the alphabet has been changed to match the patterns of arm and hand movement sequences of early childhood. It is now impossible to determine who insisted the alphabet start with "a" and follow the sequence of letters now universal. From a child development position, practice should start on the round letters that are the extensions of the circles the child learns to put on paper first. The rest of the sequence is detailed in the following instructions.

The chalkboard again becomes the best practice area. The letters should be written in large sizes. The letters like "c" and "o" should be at least six inches high, and letters like "l," "b," and "p" should be at least nine inches in size. This will assure the full arm movement so often mentioned here, and will avoid the scribbling too often seen when these letters are being put on paper. The size of the letters should not be reduced until there is the definite, observable full and fluid arm movement. Each practice session should be limited to one of the letter groups suggested below, and it is possible all letters in each group will not be accomplished in one session. You will note that the recommended sequence provides practice in similarity of the directions of movement, each new letter using some of the direction of movement found in the preceding letter. And, as in all use of the routines detailed in this book, the *quality* of the performance is much more important than the *quantity* of practice. It is better to have your child practicing for five minutes, six times a day than it is to keep at it for 30 minutes at a time with the risk of fatigue and frustration that will wipe out all the benefits of practice.

Have your child start with the first letter in Group 1, and do not urge him to proceed to the second letter until there is no apparent hesitancy in his arm and hand movements while forming the letter. Then, have him do at least four or five of the same letter in connected form so the continuity of letter to letter is practiced. This "sets in" the motor pattern for each letter. When skills are apparent for Group 1, have your child go on to Group 2. Review Group 1 before proceeding from Group 2 to Group 3. Do not hesitate to have your child review Group 1 or Group 2 after any of the advanced groups. This review will allow your child to be confident he has established the eye-hand coordinations he will need in the classroom.

Group 1. o, c, a, g, and q.

o o o   oooo

c c c   cccc

a a a   aaaa

Group 2. e, l, t, i, j, and p.

e e e   eeee

l l l   llll

Group 3. d, b, h, k, and f.

d d d   dddd

b b b   bbbb

h h h   hhhh

Group 4. m, n, and x.

m m m   mmmm

n n n   nnnn

Group 5. u, v, w, r, and s.

u u u   uuuu

v v v   vvvv

Because capital letters are individually more distinctive in shape, these should be practiced one at a time, and almost any sequence is permissible. The best results with capitals may be achieved by using letters in family names.

When the individual letters have been fully explored, and the eye-hand coordination is expressed in arm and hand fluidity, combinations of letters should be practiced. By now it would not be surprising if combinations are happening in the words your child wants to master. In any case, some practice in the following should be encouraged to reach for legibility of the letters having so many similarities. There will be many variations available on all of the above, and your child should be urged to explore these as he wishes.

Group 1. acac, adad, coco, agag, aqaq, gqgq, ococ, dada, caca, etc.

acac adad coco agag agag

Group 2. elel, ltlt, elt, tle, lele, tete, lte, let, etc.

elel ltlt elt tle

Group 3. bfbf, hkhk, bhbh, bkbk, fkfk, fhfh, bfk, kfb, fbk, etc.

bfbf hkhk bhbh bkbk

Group 4. mnmn, mrmr, mxmx, nxnx, rnrn, nmnm, rmn, nmr, nxr, rxm, etc.

mnmn mrmr mxmx

Group 5. iuiu, wuwu, vuvu, iwiw, irir, ruru, wrwr, etc.
ijij, ipip, jpjp, rsrs, sisi, susu, swsw, usis, wisi, etc.

iuiu wuwu vuvu iwiw

When all letter forms are accomplished easily and well, it is time to move to pencil and paper. The sheets of paper should be large enough to allow the same full arm and hand movements learned at the chalkboard. If these large sheets are not available, consider using the classified ads section of the daily paper. If you turn these to a horizontal position and give your child a large felt tip pen, the gray background of the fine print will cause no confusion. If sheets of newsprint are available from a newspaper office, or from a school supply store, these will be more attractive to your child.

In this first transfer from chalkboard to desk, have your child write the letters he is practicing while standing at the desk instead of being seated. This erect posture allows the duplications of the same directions of movement experienced at the chalkboard. When he is standing, up movements on the paper are more like the up movements at the chalkboard. The moment he is seated, up movements on the paper become away movements, and down movements become toward movements. The standing posture helps every child to make the transitions that must be achieved for concepts of directionality.

Now that your child is much readier to expand his eye-hand coordinations into classroom assignments, it is important for him to hold his pencil so there are none of the interfering, disruptive hand cramps. Please note in Figure 28 how the pencil should be grasped.

In all of this letter practice, there has also been the inherent practice in visual discriminations and visualization. However, now that the motor patterns are accomplished, it is time to put full emphasis upon the visual system and the exploration of its role as

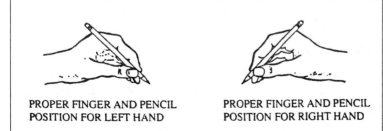

PROPER FINGER AND PENCIL
POSITION FOR LEFT HAND

PROPER FINGER AND PENCIL
POSITION FOR RIGHT HAND

Figure 28.

the dominant component in this process so significant to reading and spelling lessons. If your child is having even the least difficulty in remembering, or in spelling, or in reading comprehension, the following procedures should be explored in every possible manner. If some of these seem too juvenile for your child, find ways to sophisticate them so positive results can be obtained.

1. Place several familiar toys (or objects) on a table behind the child. Have your child turn and look at the table contents for a few seconds. Then have your child face away from the table and name as many of the toys or objects as he can recall. Gradually increase the number of toys.

2. Place several toys (or objects) on the table and have your child examine its contents for a few seconds. Have him close his eyes while you remove one. When he opens his eyes have him tell you which is missing.

These two procedures are simple, but the skill they develop is complex and important. The ability to recall what one has seen is not happenstance, and practice is necessary. This recall is not dependent upon a "good memory," but rather a good memory is the result and outgrowth of the ability to visualize something previously seen. This sort of practice is preparation for word structuring abilities. The symbols THE, THEN, THERE are examples of the addition of letters which change word context, just as No. 1 above changes the table content. Number 2 above provides similar processes of learning to subtract a letter from a word, THEIR, THEM, THE. Thus, the visual memory of things becomes practice for the visual memory of *symbols for things--words.*

3. Expose a picture out of a catalogue or magazine which contains a number of familiar items. Cover it and have your child tell as many things as he remembers seeing.

4. Pick a display of home furnishings in a furniture store window for a start. These windows will usually contain only a few items of furniture. Pause briefly before the window, instructing your child to take a good look. Walk on, or turn away, and ask your child to report as many of the displayed items as possible. It can

be a game. Mother versus child, sister versus brother--who can report the most items? Then return momentarily to the window to "check" the contents--and more important--to let each child verify his own observations.

As the skill increases, pick windows with more items displayed.

Such a game devised from routines like this could make a third grader's birthday party an unforgettable occasion for all participants!

5. Draw a simple form or pattern on your child's chalkboard while he watches you do it. Then erase it quickly and thoroughly and have him draw it as nearly like yours as possible.

6. Expose a simple pattern for a few seconds. Remove and have your child draw it from memory. First patterns shown your child should be squares, circles, triangles and rectangles of various sizes.

These give practice in the representation for form and shape. Experience in the first years of a child's life is with three-dimensional objects. The ability to transform tri-dimensional objects into bi-dimensional representations on paper is an important step in children's lives. The use of a pencil or crayon to depict the basic form of things seen involves many skill processes. This activity can give parents information concerning what and how a child sees. The more adequately a child perceives the real things around him, the better able he is to make some sort of a picture of it. Drawing is the child's method of conveying to others what things look like to him. He need not be an artist to produce such a representation, but the two skills mainly involved here (eye-hand coordination and visual memory) reach a higher level of performance through this activity. His ability to depict the slight differences between a square and a rectangle can show up later in his ability to write words of slightly different structure. His skill in visually recognizing similarities and differences of details in simple forms and shapes becomes the skill of recognition necessary for reading and spelling skills throughout the school years.

7. Print labels to place on furniture, toys and objects, have him go

from object to object with paper and pencil, copying each label. When he can do it well, remove labels and have him put on paper the word for each piece of furniture, toy or object.

Are the Labels Valid?

If your child is having difficulty with the words which label furniture, toys or other household objects, there may be a need for real emphasis on the visualization of these words. There has already been considerable discussion of the need for the integration of the visual and tactual information systems. Once more, we must realize that this process of integration reaches its ultimate level of productivity in the ability to write the word which is the representation of a person, an object or an event. There are children who become quite adept at all the verbal communications and still fail to accomplish the skills for written communications. There is a tendency to label these children dysgraphic, and to assume they cannot learn to write. Frequently, a less well informed clinician paints a very gloomy picture for the future of this child and suggests the only recourse is to depend upon a stenographer, or to try for some ability at a typewriter or word processor, whatever compensation may seem to be an acceptable substitute for the inability to write.[67]

The behavioral optometrist does not always accept such a prognosis. There are now validated tests the behavioral optometrist can use to make further appraisals of the subtle visual aspects of such problems. The clinical evidence now shows, beyond any doubt, that this sort of problem has no neurological etiology, and it is much more of a deficiency in the visualization process than anything else. It is now being mediated with carefully designed therapy procedures and the results are very positive. Children and young adults who have been dismissed as dysgraphic, for whom no help was thought available, are now demonstrating abilities in which the visual tactual reciprocities have provided the learning activities needed. There is also considerable evidence that the individuals so diagnosed missed some developmental phases and eventually became so dependent upon compensations that what ability they might have had to write was sublimated and forgotten in favor of other less difficult methods of communication.[65,2,44,51]

If your child is having a problem learning to write when his peers are succeeding in this activity, the following procedure can be significantly important to his progress. Of course, the alphabet practice routines must be used as introduction to this procedure.

8. If your child can write any word, have him put it on the chalkboard in very large letters in cursive form. If he cannot write the word for himself, write it for him in a size that almost fills the entire board horizontally, with letters at least six to nine inches in vertical dimensions. As with the alphabet, this will assure he gets all possible kinesthetic and proprioceptive signals out of his arm and hand actions. Now have him trace over the word several times, saying each letter aloud as each is formed. Observe the continuity and fluidity of your child's arm-hand movements as he traces, and as soon as you see no hesitancy in either the sequence or formation of each letter, have him step back about three feet away from the chalkboard. He is now to pretend his chalk is three feet long so he can again trace each letter in the air, as if he were still writing on the board. If the continuity is still observable, and he vocalizes each letter in the word without any hesitancy, ask him to close his eyes, to "see" the word in his mind as he once again traces it in the air. If his movements and vocalizations are still fluid and continuous, have him face away from the chalkboard and with his eyes open write the word on an imaginary chalkboard in front of him. Now have him close his eyes and, while "seeing" the word in his mind, spell it aloud for you. Urge him to make every possible effort to visualize the word at all times. You will have clues to his ability to do this by watching how accurately he dots the "i", or crosses the "t", which may occur in the chosen word. If he cannot accurately place the dot or cross, the chances are he is not visualizing clearly and the entire procedure should be repeated. Any errors or hesitancy in any step of the procedure are reasons to go back to the original tracing on the chalkboard. Finally, to be sure he has learned to write this word, and to "set in" his visualization of it, have him now write it on paper.

This routine should be used on every word with which your child has any difficulty. It not only establishes writing abilities, it is a very successful method for the mediation of spelling problems, and

Figure 29. Writing in the air as your child "traces his visualization of a word" is another manner of learning that a word can feel like it looks and looks just like it feels. This is one of the most productive steps to spelling skills.

many children have moved up to A's in spelling after they have learned to visualize, and to "set in" the word by writing it. Your attention is called to the number of learning systems brought into this procedure. Here there is the proprioception for movement patterns, the verbalization for auditory reinforcements, the visualization for both short term and long term memory support, and the visible result of the interweavings of all these systems in the word that can be seen on the board and on paper. At least six learning systems have been integrated: arm and hand movements, the tactual signals of the chalk drag on the board, the sound of the chalk and the stimulus to audition, the use of the voice, the visually directed and monitored hand movements, and the mental imagery of the entire process. The learning process is always enhanced by the integration of relevant systems, and the more systems that can be included in an act, the greater the cognitive result for the development of intelligence. It now appears that one major reason for a diagnosis of dysgraphia lies in the inability of the individual to automatically integrate all relevant systems. The procedure just described guides the child to such integrations, and individuals so incorrectly diagnosed no longer fit the label given them.[29]

Imagination, creativity, innovativeness and the ability to anticipate what one wishes to do in the future are all abilities found only in the human. Daydreaming and imagination are very positive childhood activities and need to be utilized and encouraged by parents. Needless to say, excessive daydreaming and fabrication should not be allowed, but the child's own use of visualizations into speech (and later into drawing and creative writing) can well determine his adult future. A dress designer, an architect, an artist, and anyone else who must plan ahead in chosen projects, depends entirely upon visualization skills to assure economy and effectiveness of actions.

IS YOUR CHILD AN OBSERVER OR A PARTICIPANT?

Our culture has provided too many substitutes for the pretend play of childhood. Boys are expected to move into sports as early as possible, and the playground does not offer much chance for pretense. Little girls are reporting that doll play and imitating mother are "sissy" activities and they, too, are expected to be as successful on the sports field as their brothers. As a result, too many children are observers of others instead of participants in the activities which develop the visualization abilities. The ability to pretend participation in an interesting story being read will determine the level of comprehension achieved.

Since visualizations are initially based upon actual experiences, parents should be aware of all the opportunities there are to guide children into visualization skills that become the basis for anticipation and creativity. These, like intelligence, have inherent potentials, but the degree of sophistication one achieves here is acquired just as cultural intelligence is acquired--by the practice which will enhance the potentials. Following are suggestions for the development of these advanced visual abilities.

1. Describe something and have your child name it from your description. "I am thinking of something big and green, with four doors and four wheels, and windows all around, that is used every day to go places," etc. Have your child try to visualize it while the object is being described and then add his further descriptions of it.

2. Describe the clothes and appearance of a playmate or member of the family until your child can name who is being described.

3. Describe a place in town like a park, a store, or Grandmother's house until your child can name it. Then have your child tell about it, what he does there, who lives or plays or works there, etc. This will assist him to visualize it. If he mixes or confuses places, people and things, correct him with descriptive details so his visual projections can be more accurate.

4. Have your child tell about the trip he made with you to the grocery store. Question and lead him into details of the store and its contents.

5. Have your child find objects in stores which he has seen on the TV commercials. As he watches the commercials have him tell you which store has the objects and what part of the store they were in.

6. Have your child tell you how to get from his own house to someone else's home in detail; and tell who lives in between, with attention to the places such as churches, schoolhouse, parks, etc. that are on the route.

7. While riding in the car have your child tell which corners to turn to get to your destination.

8. After using the usual routes from one place to another have your child describe the route to you as if he were making the trip. When he becomes capable of doing so have him learn new routes and describe them also. During talk time have him tell you how to get to other places as though he were making the trip.

9. Have your child tell about places that are not familiar everyday trips--such as places visited on a vacation trip, what was done there, who was visited and some of the details he saw while there.

10. While sitting at the dinner table have your child close his eyes and point to things on the table, such as the bread, potatoes, his plate, Mother's plate, Father's chair, etc. If he makes an error, have him open his eyes and correct himself. This is the game of "Where Is It?"

11. Send your child on errands around the house, but before he goes after the object desired, have him tell you where it is located.

12. Have him describe and locate the furniture in other rooms of the house without going there. If he makes errors, have him go look and return with correct descriptions.

13. Have your child tell you what pictures are on the walls in his room, or the pattern of the wallpaper, etc.

14. Have your child count or name rows of objects from left to right. Count and name by pointing with finger, then count and name with eyes alone. Finally repeat with eyes closed.

15. Urge your child to draw pictures--simple line drawings--of his house, toys and playmates. Large sheets of paper (wrapping paper, newsprint paper, etc.) are most suitable for the young child. Urge him to draw as he wishes, but always find an opportunity to have him tell you about his drawing.

The child who reports the first robin in the spring, who picks the first colorful fall leaf for his teacher, and who breathlessly reports an exciting view or occurrence to his mother, is the child who sees his world and its wonders. This is the observant child--the child who visually probes and explores his surroundings. This is truly a wonderful ability because out of these childhood awarenesses comes the adult skill of "sizing up the situation in a glance." The skill of being observant can be established so easily by parents if proper starting points and sequences are used. It is of frequent value in this full and speedy world. Most adults miss so much of what goes on around them because they lack width of vision. The shrewd lawyer in every whodunit written wins his case on this adult deficiency. All of the procedures just described will also assist your child to be more observant and visually aware of his world.

READING--THE MOST COMPLEX OF ALL HUMAN ABILITIES

This section should not be closed without a little further consideration of the complexities in learning to read. There are some children who have difficulty gaining mastery of reading even after working at all of the procedures recommended in the preceding pages.

Careful educational and optometric examinations show that these children have gained all the skills and readinesses that are essential to reading ability. Still they read only what they are forced to read and do this very poorly. Because these children pass the usual tests, their inability is blamed upon a lack of motivation or a lack of self-application. It just does not seem reasonable that the normally curious, eager-to-learn child is not attracted to the information that he can obtain through reading. Oddly enough, this situation occurs most frequently among children in the first three grades, where the skills for learning to read must be achieved if a child is to use reading for learning in the following grades. While taking case histories on these children, many optometrists have asked them about school, what subjects are easy for them, what subjects they like and what subjects are difficult. Many first and second graders, during this conversation with the optometrist, spontaneously report their dislike for reading. Careful questioning of these children has brought out a very frequent and surprising universal reason for the dislike they have expressed. Their comments--"My cat's name is not Boots" or "I don't know anyone named Richard"--very significantly indicate that the stories they have in first and second grade readers are not related to their own background of experience. Many excellent teachers have attempted to counteract this strange and unrealistic material with group participation in daily experience reading exercises. The teacher will ask what day it is; several of the children will answer, and while "This is Tuesday" is being put on the chalkboard, the rest of the class are probably still wondering "What difference does it make what day it is." This should not be interpreted as condemnation of the experience reader technique. The question being raised here concerns its value as a group activity where clinical practice has shown its greater value as an individual activity. Just because several children in a classroom are capable of telling what day it might be does not mean that the rest of the children in the room have had a background into which this bit of information can be fitted. In spite of this criticism, which is sincerely meant to be analytical and constructive, teachers should not discontinue this part of their classroom procedure. Parents should recognize that the experience reader technique can also be used by them to supplement the classroom activity, and at the same time to encourage their child's interest and curiosity in the written word.

The use of this procedure applied to their own child's experiences and events of his individual day helps him to realize the value of writing and reading as important means of communication. Furthermore, writing and reading are the ultimate procedures in concept formation.[80,21,20,5,51,29,81,37,9,19,82,83,84]

A detailed analysis of having a child write short sentences about his own experiences gives insight to the reasons why so many children have profited when parents used this method of helping their child learn to read.

a. The memories and visualizations of the events of the day about which he talks let him practice recall and the organization of the sequence of the day's occurrences.

b. The language he uses and his choice of words out of his own vocabulary lets him apply the words most meaningful to him.

c. The places, people and things he puts into his story are all very realistic to him--unless he goes into flights of fancy, which parents will immediately recognize. If this does occur, a bit of the same steering suggested in the section on language in this book will bring your child back to reality.

d. The dictation (or writing) of these words and his memory of the account will assist a child to visually recognize the words when he reads the sentences.

e. The procedure will help a child to realize that "readin' is just talkin' wrote down." When a child realizes, as he will, that he is readin' his own talkin', he is usually very pleased over the fact that he can recognize his own words. Parents have frequently reported that their child was so fascinated by these words out of his own mouth that reading sessions ceased to be the dreaded chore and were demanded by the child. Many children have changed from the poorest reader in their class to one of the best readers in the group by this method.

The following procedures have proven to be effective with most children in helping them to match their visualizations to printed words.

1. Have your child dictate in his own words short sentence ac-

counts of his day to you. It is best that this be done when he comes in from school or before the evening meal. Type it for him if possible. If a typewriter is not available, print it or write it in the same sort of letters used by his teacher at school.

2. Have him immediately read it back to you while it is all fresh in his mind. Help him with the words he stumbles on, discuss the word, and the event or item being described so his concept of the word is complete.

3. Put this paper into a notebook and lay it away until evening when he again reads it before going to bed.

4. Repeat this activity each day, adding each new page to the notebook. Have your child reread and review previously written pages and urge him to increase the length of his stories as his vocabulary and word recognition skills increase. Help him to increase his accuracy of word usage as his skills increase but do not be too demanding until after your child finds out that this activity can be fun as well as instructive.

5. As the stories increase in length, decrease the number of pages used for review. When the stories become more complete and your child becomes more fluent in his account, encourage him to start writing part of the story himself. This can be done by having him write some of the sentences or leave spaces for him to fill with words he is capable of writing.

6. As your child gains facility in writing, utilize the chalkboard as much as possible for word practice. The skills of full arm movements developed by previous chalkboard routines will be apparent in your child's writing.

7. If, for any reason, this method of bringing your child's visualizations to the printed page does not seem to help or does not hold his interest, it can easily be expanded into a more intimate activity which assures the greater participation of your child. Obtain the simplest and least expensive automatic camera. The Kodak Instamatic is the best example of these. This camera can be mastered by very young, and even retarded, children because it demands very little instructions in its use. Load it with a 12-exposure cartridge; DO NOT begin with the 20-exposure

cartridge. Have your child take a series of pictures of his choosing, but try to arrange it so the series is about a single event--such as a family picnic, a trip to the beach, or a visit to a relative. Help him to get the series started as you are leaving your home. Include activities which explain the event and then, perhaps, show the return home. Send the film off for developing and plan for a time lapse of several days. This time lapse is important for memory practice and the one hour developers, or Polaroid instant cameras, should not be used because they are too instantaneous for the practice in remembering.

When the prints are available, have your child sort them in the sequence in which he took the pictures. As he does this sorting, urge him to use these illustrations to jog his memories of the event. As soon as this is accomplished with a reasonable degree of skill in recall, now ask him to dictate something about each picture--who is in the picture, what they are doing, and all the relevancies he can describe which are illustrated in the pictures. Use this dictated material in the fashion described above.

The second time such a series of pictures is taken of a family event, have your child carefully choose six out of the 12 pictures that provide ample illustration of the event. Again, he dictates and develops his own experience reader about his own experience.

On following occasions, have your child choose the three pictures out of the 12 that are adequate and appropriate illustrations of the events. The challenge of choosing three out of 12 pictures will demand he carefully make visual inspections of each picture and the visual discriminations of the pertinency of each of the pictures. At the same time, he is challenged to verbalize around and beyond each picture to be sure his story is complete while being fully illustrated by such a few pictures. This provides practice in seeing more than a picture actually contains by expanding the context of the picture with his choice of words. It has frequently been said that a good picture is worth 10,000 words. This is only true if the viewer has the words to bring to the picture AND the picture is good enough to trigger the visualizations which can then be put into 10,000 words. When your child takes the pictures that illustrate his stories, the relevancies which are inherent in such a procedure make the 10,000 words--or even 1,000 words--more of a possibility.

If you will pick up a primary reader you will likely find it has been illustrated with pictures representing the artist's interpretation of the content, rather than containing illustrations children can accept as realistic representations of their experiences. The books which attract and hold your child's interest are most likely those in which he can participate through the visualizations he brings to them, and their pictures, out of his own background. As in the previous discussions on the development of vision language patterns, the routines just recommended provide another example of how "readin' is jist talkin' wrote down." One might even hope your child would be challenged enough by these routines to prepare a full book of words and pictures about a family vacation trip across the nation, or a visit to a beautiful National Park. Now, all the magic of being able to write and read can bring your child to the most available sources of limitless information--all the books our culture now provides to anyone who wishes them.

The application of these procedures carried through to the stages where your child shows the acquisition of visual discrimination abilities will prove to be most helpful routines for almost every child. Some children will be too old, or too young, for some particular activity, but the alert parent will find adaptations and variations where these suggestions can be applied to the proper level.

Older children can be encouraged to utilize "young" routines by having them teach and demonstrate the activities to younger children. The important thing is to realize that the most commonplace, simple, everyday activity can be used to develop the skills so necessary to meet the demands of our culture and the child's school life.

We parents must always remember that it is possible to expect too much of a child. Do not push into advanced activities until your child has mastered the basic procedures. Occasional review of the entire sequence of activities assures his organization of all skills. Review is especially indicated when mastery of advanced skills is difficult or inadequate. When the sequences of growth and development and the sequences of training are in keeping with each other, the results of any practice are much greater.

CHAPTER V
THE SCHOOL YEARS

Most of today's parents expect their children to spend at least 12 nine-month periods within a school environment. The importance of these years is well recognized by everyone, but the past few years have been filled with comments, articles, speeches and even books--all discussing what is wrong with our educational system. This atmosphere of criticism has brought condemnation of teachers by parents--and condemnation of parents by teachers.

As painful as it may be, we parents will have to admit that most of the blame will have to rest upon our shoulders. We have let our children come to school age without meeting our responsibility in developing readiness and basic skills. We have frequently heard, "Teachers do not want us to teach our child anything; they want to do it at school." Teachers are reasonable and correct in desiring that parents do not attempt to teach school subjects before the school years, but teachers are also reasonable and correct in their desire that children come to the first grades with ability to button their clothing, tie shoelaces and get along with other children. Many kindergarten teachers must spend school time developing these abilities the children should have achieved before school entrance. In these respects we parents have failed the child AND the teacher. We cannot, and must not, expect teachers to do our jobs for us.

The parent-child-teacher triangle has been a difficult one. Perhaps this difficulty has existed because of a lack of communication at the adult levels. No sincere parent wants special privileges for his child, and no sincere teacher will deprive any child of his rightful privileges in the schoolroom. If the adults in this triangle will give a bit more consideration to their unique responsibilities to the child, and then communicate with each other regarding the manner in which these responsibilities can be fulfilled, every child will benefit. Teachers should tell parents where they can assist a child, not in the application of schoolroom methods as homework drills, but in the related skill developments such as recommended in this book. Nearly every teacher, knowing children as well as she does, will be able to point out to parents many of the routines given within these pages which will assist the child to better achievement in the classroom. Parents should stand ready to take these suggestions and thus assist the child to apply what he learns in school to his everyday extracurricular activities.

Parents should also know what is expected of their child at each grade level. Perhaps education has been a bit neglectful in not passing on to parents some sort of a grade-by-grade outline of these expecteds. Such an outline is now available. Folded into the back of this book is a chart made up by educators who have drawn from the fields of child development and educational psychology. It was made available to all teachers in Sonoma County, California, and is titled "Growth and Development Through the Grades." This illustrates, on age and grade levels, the abilities a child must possess for success in the primary grades of our educational system. This chart* is included in this book as a guide to parents so they can determine their child's readiness for each grade. Used thus, parents can check their child's abilities against what the school expects. Used in conjunction with the routines in the previous pages, every parent should be able to integrate his guidance and training for the child with the sequences of academic training a child must meet in the schoolroom.

In this fashion, growth and development, training and guidance can all become a means of communication between parents and teachers, as well as a method of acquiring higher achievement levels for every child.

*Our thanks to the County Superintendent of Schools, Sonoma, California, for permission to reprint this chart.

POSTSCRIPT

This book illustrates how the child's world is built by HIM. Parents, teachers and clinicians can set the stage, but only the child himself can act thereon. A child is taught nothing--he learns everything--and vision is the supreme mechanism a child possesses for the interpretation of his world. All other mechanisms discussed here are important for a "total child," but they are all subservient to vision.

The emphasis on vision in this book does not result from the author's professional interest or prejudice. This emphasis is the consequence of the dire need for a better understanding on the part of all who guide and care for children.

The following authorities in related disciplines have all made comments pertinent to this subject.

Gesell states: "Vision is the dominant factor in human development."

Halstead states: "We cannot speak of vision AND intelligence--they are one and the same thing."

Renshaw states: "Vision is made up of the tendons, muscles and the articular surfaces of the joints," and "Vision is learned."

Walls states: "Vision is the product of a very simple eye and a very complex brain."

Harmon states: "The child strives to grow, develop and function as an integrated whole. Each of its responses to the forces of its environment have a large share in determining the child's later developments, efficiencies and well-being."

This book has been written with one main purpose--to convey to parents the importance of the learning activities of children and to present simple, positive suggestions for child guidance. The more extensive the parental understanding of the processes involved, the greater the possibilities for all children.

Visual memory, visual comparison, visual projection and visual imagination, visual localization and visual discrimination of likes and differences are all involved and basic to the performance of every activity suggested here. Vision is involved in every meaningful learning activity.

Thus, vision training is intelligence training.

You, as a parent, hold it within your power to provide your child with the opportunity for success in school through the development of his visual skills. These can be developed and extended through your guidance with the supervision and professional skill of the behavioral optometrist. His optometric training and his knowledge of visual performance and visual achievement and child development, plus your parental love and interest, can complete the combination that will make your child's tomorrows as full and as intellectually rich as they should be.

> Sow a thought and reap a purpose.
> Sow a purpose and reap an action.
> Sow an action and reap a habit.
> Sow a habit and reap a character.
> Sow a character and reap a destiny.
> --*Tyrone Edwards*

APPENDIX

A search of the literature on child development, intellectual development and educational methods can be a never-ending process. Probably no other subjects, except religion, have had as much published about them, and this search cannot ever explore all the books one could find. It is not difficult, however, to pick out references and remarks that illustrate the common thread of opinions and interpretations that run through all the literature. It is interesting that even where there is considerable disagreement on methods of rearing and education of children, there is much agreement on the basic concepts of human development and how it can be hindered, or enhanced, depending upon cultural and environmental influences.

One could fill a large book with such references and remarks. Perhaps a few of these will help every reader of this book to gather a little of the background which has been brought to summation in this publication. The comments chosen are from representatives of education, pediatrics, ophthalmology, psychology and optometry, with selections made on the basis of pertinency, and status of the person being quoted. Each will be identified thus (e) for education, (p) for pediatrics, (o) for ophthalmology, (psy) for psychology and (opt) for optometry. Please note the dates on each of the items since these will give an idea of the long-standing interest in what has been presented in this book.

Life is a succession of lessons that must be lived to be understood. Experience, and not memory, is the mother of ideas. My desire is to impress all with the importance of developing the organism through each of the different sense channels, in addition to the verbal or word centers. The tendency with the present modes of education is to overtax the memory and overload the mind with studied words. Instruction by telling is a feeble mode of impressing the mind. 'Actions speak louder than words.' Only in proportion to my experience can I understand the symbols for things, that is, words. Words are empty sounds unless accompanied by clear ideas or thoughts of the things signified. I can have true ideas or false ideas only in proportion to my experience.

From: New Methods in Education, by J. Liberty Tadd. Orange Judd Company, New York, 1902: 16 (e)

The human organism strives to grow, develop and function as an integrated whole. In each of its responses to the forces or restraints in its environment which stimulate it, it performs organically by seeking physical balances with those forces and restraints which meet certain functions on inherently determined system of coordinates. These responses have a large share in determining the organism's later developments, efficiencies, and well-being.

From: The Coordinated Classroom, by Darrell Boyd Harmon. American Institute of Architects, File No. 35-B, 1942 (psy & e)

Some of the earliest literature on visual-tactual integrations (frequently referred to as 'the kinesthetic methods') appeared in the reports of Plato (427-347 BC) in 'Protagoras.' Here he describes the early stages of learning to write.'When a boy is not yet clever in writing, the masters first draw lines, and then give him a tablet and make him write as the lines direct.' Quintilian (about 68 AD) recommended: 'As soon as the child has begun to know the shapes of the various letters, it will be no bad thing to have them cut as accurately as possible upon a board, so that the pen may be guided along the grooves. Thus mistakes such as occur with wax tablets will be rendered impossible, for the pen will be confined between the edges of the letters and will be prevented from going astray.' Quintilian further advised: 'learning the sound and the form of the letters simultaneously'."

From: Remedial Techniques in Basic School Subjects, by Grace M. Fernald, McGraw-Hill Book Company, 1943: 27 (psy)

Perhaps the most important conclusion to be drawn from the extensive researches here reported is that disability of any degree in any of the basic school subjects is wholly preventable. If educational methods were more intelligently adapted to the idiosyncrasies of the individual child, all children would achieve up to their mental level in all school subjects. It is largely for this reason that I believe this book is one of the most significant contributions ever made to experimental pedagogy.

Foreword written by Prof. Lewis Terman, of Stanford University, in the book by Grace Fernald, 1943: ix (psy & e)

Discrimination is a process of differentiation; perception is a higher level process of recognition. For example, visual discrimination is a prerequisite to the visual perception, or recognition, of the words in the reading process. A pupil who can discriminate between the forms of words is a good observer. Some children, for some reason or combination of reasons, do not make accurate observations regarding the likes and differences between word forms. Visual discrimination is based upon trained observational skills."

From: Foundations of Reading Instruction, by Emmett Albert Betts. American Book Company, 1946: 330 (e)

Comparable social forces are beginning to define the possibilities and opportunities of professional specialization in the field of child vision. The child specialist in this area will have a basic scientific interest in the nature and needs of child development. He will relate his practice to the broader aspects of family and child welfare, as well as to specific visual difficulties; he will recognize the pervasive mechanisms of growth in his policy of periodic follow-up; he will adjust treatment and guidance to these mechanisms; he will appreciate that vision lies close to the citadel of personality, and will so render his services that the dignity of the individual child will be respected. This he will do through deepened insight into the general dynamics of growth which underlie the patterning of individuality in vision.

From: Vision, Its Development in Infant and Child, by Arnold Gesell et al. Paul B. Hoeber, 1949: 294 (p)

It is our belief that motion and perception are inseparably related, the development of perception in the child is the development of motion, and the only valid understanding of perception at any level is in terms of the movements that define it ....The organization and stability of the perceptual field depend on movements of orientation, location, and differential manipulations that have become established in the motion patterns of the individual.

From: Perception and Motion, by Smith and Smith. W. B. Saunders Co., 1962: 7 (psy)

It should be remembered that biologically the eyes were adapted for relatively simple purposes--to look for enemies and for food; and although, from long custom, we accept the conditions in which we live today as normal, it by no means follows that the eyes have evolved sufficiently to fulfill the exorbitant demands of unremitting close work imposed upon them by a highly complex and artificial civilization. The more is this understandable when we remember the functional minutiae required for the attainment of accurate vision and the high degree of coordination necessary between the movements of the two eyes so they will fulfill the requirements of binocular vision. It is understandable that this complexity of the visual apparatus tends to make it less capable of withstanding long-continued strain than a cruder and less highly specialized mechanism.

From: Ophthalmic Optics and Refraction, Vol. V, Chapter XV, by Sir Stewart Duke-Elder. C. V. Mosby, St. Louis, 1970: 559 (o)

Visual exercises: We have already seen in the fourth volume of this series of texts that vision includes not only the formation of retinal images by the dioptric system of the eyes and their transference by physiological processes to the cortex (of the brain), but also the perceptual appreciation of their presentation as patterns endowed with meaning. In the interpretation of such patterns the memories of past experience play a dominant part and the ease and efficiency of the process of seeing depends in a very large measure on the facilitation of the cortical processes involved. Orthodox ophthalmology has devoted itself almost entirely to the events occurring at the lower level, and has confined its interest to the means of attaining suitable dioptric images on corresponding retinal areas to the relative exclusion of the consideration of events at the higher level; and it must be admitted that this unequal division of interest is without reason! Difficulties of interpretation at the higher level can be as much a cause of strain as (optical) disturbances at the lower, and in the easement of visual strain the ophthalmologist should give consideration to them both. The facilitation of the processes of seeing is exemplified in a comparison between the efforts of a child who fixes each letter in his early attempts at reading with the practiced reader who can interpret print with a glance which does not require fixation even on each word; it is the difference between the facile ease of the practiced golfer or skater and the strained efforts of the tiro ....Repetitive exercises, by facilitation of the perceptual processes and the provision of an accumulated fund of memories and associations to aid interpretation, are of an immense aid in the art of seeing.

From: *Ophthalmic Optics and Refraction, Vol. V, Chapter XV, by Sir Stewart Duke-Elder. C. V. Mosby, St. Louis, 1970: 575-576 (o)*

Therefore, the inherent responsibilities that are assumed by every adult who is guiding children, demand that only the best and most thorough care and guidance be given the child. If this responsibility is shirked, or ignored, to any degree in any of these observations, then both the teacher and the child will suffer the consequences. The teacher's daily load will be heavier and less productive--and in some cases, complete failure! The child's daily load will be more difficult and discouraging and, in time, may become so discouraging to him that he no longer tries to succeed in the visual process of learning to read. The early identification of any interfering visual problem can be the difference between success or failure for both the child and the teacher in the total educational process.

From: *Learning to See and Seeing to Learn. "The Early Identification of the Interfering Visual Problem," by G. N. Getman. Mafex Associates, 1971: 123 (opt)*

Robinson (1953) reported that the only visual scores which

consistently differentiated high and low achievers (in reading) involved binocular visual performance. It is interesting to note that Beltman et al. (1967), in their study of dyslexia reported that 42% of the dyslexics and only 9% of the controls failed their simple foveal suppression tests. Yet, they concluded this finding was NOT significant. Benton (1973) reports five times the incidence of convergence difficulties in the learning-disabled population as compared to the normal. In the literature on vision and learning one very definite trend becomes apparent. Those who considered the physiological as well as the physical visual processes found relationships to exist between vision and learning. Those who restricted their testing largely to the physical segment found there was little or no relationship between vision and learning. However, all state that they were APPRAISING VISION."

From: Basic Visual Process and Learning Disability, by Gerald Leisman. Charles Thomas Co., 1976, Chapter 14: 333 (e)

Vision is developed by the growing child as a result of the child interacting with his environment. The process of this development has been carefully documented by numerous researchers and clinicians (Gesell, 1949; Getman, 1962; Piaget, 1969). Their studies leave little doubt that VISION IS A LEARNED SKILL. Its development has been shown to follow the same laws of anatomical, physiological and psychological development as all other learned skills, and therefore is subject to the same developmental inadequacies. Visual system inadequacies can lead to visual problems, which, in turn, may affect the learning process.

From: Basic Visual Processes and Learning Disability, by Gerald Leisman. Charles Thomas Co., 1976, Chapter 19: 393 (e)

The development of vision in the individual child is complex because it took countless ages of evolution in the race to bring vision to its present advanced state. Human visual perception ranks with speech in complexity and passes through comparable developmental phases. Moreover, seeing is not a separate, isolable function; it is profoundly integrated with the total action system of the child, his posture, his manual skills and coordination, intelligence, and even his personality make-up. 'Indeed, vision is so intimately identified with the whole child that we cannot understand its economy and its hygiene without investigating the whole child.'(Gesell, 1949) Vision, therefore, may be the key to a fuller understanding of the nature and needs of the individual child. He sees with his whole being. The conservation of vision, particularly in the young child, goes far beyond the detection and correction of 'refractive errors.' Acuity is only one part and aspect of the economy of vision.

From: Basic Visual Processes and Learning Disability, by Gerald Leisman. Charles Thomas Co., 1976, Chapter 19: 394 (e)

What complicates the diagnosis of the learning-disabled child and can be accomplished to help this child visually are two questions which must be answered. Confusion regarding vision and sight will continue to exist because many educators, psychologists, pediatricians and others in the medical profession equate vision solely with refractive errors and reduced visual acuity. On the other hand, many optometrists consider a model of vision which incorporates the perceptual, developmental and integrative aspects along with the simple end-organ functions of acuity, fixation, accommodation, convergence and fusion (Rappaport, 1967).

From: Basic Visual Processes and Learning Disability, by Gerald Leisman. Charles Thomas Co., 1976, Chapter 19: 405 (e)

Just as there must be a recognition of the interrelationships of the information systems within the total child, there must be a recognition of the interrelationships of the sources of information now available. Just as none of the information systems in the child can be considered in isolation, neither can the information sources be considered in isolation. This concept (of interdisciplinary communication) is not new by any means, but although it is frequently expressed, it has yet to be very frequently implemented because of the reluctance of so many in some disciplines to either listen to, or read, the philosophies of other disciplines. I learned long ago that I eventually profit the most by directing myself to read and examine the comments of those with whom I do NOT agree. If we can all begin to do this, new and positive vistas will be opened to such as those of us contributing to this book--but more especially to every child we will be influencing, either directly or indirectly (Getman, 1976).

From: Teaching Children with Learning Disabilities, by Kaufman and Hallahan. Charles E. Merrill, 1978, Chapter 7: 234 (e)

Departure from the traditional disease model. By dealing with a child's strengths and styles, the pediatrician, or health care professional, deviates from the traditional disease orientation. For example, one might 'diagnose' particularly superior motor skills in a child and then suggest ways such an asset can be utilized. This requires a departure from the deficit-oriented medical model.

From: A Pediatric Approach to Learning Disorders, by Levine, Brooks and Shonkoff. Wiley and Sons, 1980, Chapter 1: 12 (p)

If we confine our attention to activity involving physical interaction with the environment, or objects in it (that is, ignoring such activities as verbal communication), it is clear that vision is the most powerful exteroceptive sense. No one would, I suppose, dispute this. What I want to argue, however, is that vision is also the most powerful proprioceptive and exproprioceptive sense. Further, because of its trimodal power, vision normally functions as an overseer in the control of activity, developing patterns of action, and turning up other perceptual systems and keeping them tuned.

From: The Functions of Vision, by D. N. Lee. In: Modes of Perceiving and Processing Information, Edited by H. L. Pick, Jr. and Elliott Saltzman. John Wiley & Sons, 1983: 361 (psy)

The help-children-to-learn, carefully prescribed preventive, learning lenses for use in the classroom are irreplaceable. This is the only thing that will satisfy the avoidance response to school-task containment. With the educator using present knowledge of developing visual perception in children, and the behavioral optometrist applying his clinical knowledge to prevent visual problems that interfere with learning, there is the possibility of developing a generation of adults capable of fully utilizing their intellectual endowments. These superior adults will fulfill the exacting demands of our developing technical age.

From: A. M. Skeffington writings published by the Optometric Extension Program Foundation, 1928 to 1984 (opt)

Notes

Notes

References

1. Almy M, Chittenden E, Miller P. Young children's thinking. New York: Teachers' College Press, Columbia University, 1967.
2. Bode HB. How we learn. Boston: D. C. Heath & Co., 1940.
3. Frank LK. Human development, an emerging scientific discipline. In Introductory Section, Solnit & Provence, Modern Perspectives in child development. New York: International Universities Press, Inc., 1965.
4. Piaget J. The language and thought of the child. London: Routledge & Kegan Paul, 1926-1952.
5. Elkind D. Studies in cognitive development. Essays in honor of Jean Piaget. Flavell JH, (Ed.). London: Oxford University Press, 1969.
6. Gibson JW. The perception of the visual world. New York: Houghton & Mifflin, 1950.
7. Grasseli R, Hegner P. Playful parenting. New York: Richard Marek, 1981.
8. Halstead W. Brain and intelligence. Chicago: Chicago University Press, 1947.
9. Hunt J. Mc. Intelligence and experience. New York: Ronald Press, 1961.
10. Ittelson WH, Cantril H. Perception. New York: Random House, 1954.
11. Koffa K. The growth of the mind. Humanities Press, 1924.
12. Piaget J. The child's conception of the world. London: Humanities Press, 1951.
13. Riesen AH. The development of perception in man and chimpanzee. Science, 1947: 106 -108.
14. Stephens B (Ed.) Training the developmentally young. New York: John Day Co., 1971.
15. Strauss AA, Lehtinen LE. The psychopathology and education of the brain-injured child, Vol. I. New York: Grune & Stratton, 1951.
16. Strauss AA, Kephart NC. The psychopathology and education of the brain-injured child, Vol. II. New York: Grune & Stratton, 1955.
17. Wheeler RH, Perkins FT. Principles of mental development. New York: Thomas Crowell & Co., 1932.
18. Gesell A et al. Infant and child in the culture of today (1943), The embryology of human behavior (1945), The child from 5 to 10 (1946), Vision, its development in infant and child (1949). New York: Harper and Brothers, all publications.
19. Kelley EC. Education for what is real. New York: Harper & Bros., 1947.
20. Bruner JS, Goodman CG. Value and need as organizing factors in perception. J Abnorm Soc Psych, Jan. 1947, Vol. 42, No. 1.
21. Birch HG. Reading disability. J. Money (Ed.) Baltimore: The Johns Hopkins Press, Chapter 10, 1962.
22. Goodenough FL. Measurement of intelligence by drawings. New York: World Book Co., 1926.
23. Lyons CV, Lyons EB. The power of visual training, Part 1. J Am Optom Assoc, 1954: 255-262.
24. Lyons CV, Lyons EB. The power of visual training, Part 2. J Am Optom Assoc, November 1956.
25. Renshaw S. Psychological optics. Optom Extension Prog, 1940- 1955.
26. Terman LM, Merrill MA. Measuring intelligence. New York: Houghton & Mifflin, 1937.
27. Wilcox B. Helping children learn. New York: Vantage Press, 1975.
28. Getman GN, Gesell A. Vision, its development in infant and child. New York: Harper & Bros., 1949.
29. Getman GN. The visuomotor complex in the acquisition of learning skills. In Learning disorders, Vol. 1. Seattle: Special Child Publications, 1965.
30. Skeffington AM. Lectures and papers. Optom Extension Prog, 1926-1978.

31. Vernon MD. A further study of visual perception. London: Cambridge University Press, 1952.
32. Betts EA, Hackman RB. An evaluation of the Baltimore Myopia Project. J Am Optom Assoc, March 1957.
33. Lovgren GK. The art of inner seeing. Arizona: Karl Bern, Publishers, 1977.
34. Lyons EB. How to use your power of visualization. Marshall, Calif: Golden Rule Printing Co., 1980.
35. Harmon DB. Some preliminary observations on the developmental problems of 160,000 elementary school children. Med Women's J, March 1942.
36. Betts EA. Foundations of reading instruction. New York: American Book Co., 1946.
37. Greenstein T (Ed.) Vision and learning disability. J Am Optom Assoc, 1976.
38. Wold R. (Ed.) Visual and perceptual aspects for the achieving and underachieving child. Seattle: Special Child Publications, 1969.
39. Wold R. Vision, its impact on learning. Seattle: Special Child Publications, 1978.
40. Montessori M. The Montessori Manual. Translated by Dorothy Canfield Fisher. W. E. Richardson Co., 1913.
41. Orem RC (Ed.) The Montessori Manual, Dr. Montessori's own handbook. New York: G. P. Putnam & Sons, 1965.
42. Vurpillot E. The visual world of the child. New York: University Press, 1976.
43. Barbe WB, Francis AS, Braun LA. Spelling. Columbus, Ohio: The Zaner-Bloser Co., 1982.
44. Fernald GM. Remedial techniques in basic school subjects. New York: McGraw Hill, 1943.
45. Kauffman JM, Hallahan DP. Teaching children with learning disabilities, personal perspectives. Columbus, Ohio: Merrill Publishing Co., 1976.
46. Leisman G (Ed.). Basic visual processes and learning disability. Springfield, Ill.: Charles Thomas, 1976.
47. Monroe M, Backen B. Remedial reading. New York: Houghton Mifflin, 1937.
48. Orem RC (Ed.). Learning to see, seeing to learn. Johnstown, Penn.: Mafex Associates, 1971.
49. Walter WG. The living brain. New York: W. W. Norton & Co., 1953.
50. Getman GN. The developmental concept applied to vision training. Optom Extension Prog, November 1952.
51. Getman GN. Studies in visual development (privately published, 1954), Studies in perceptual development (privately published, 1955). Published for Invitational Seminars, Purdue University, 1954-1958.
52. Getman GN. The child as a total organism. Author's monograph, 1949.
53. Smith KU, Smith WM. Perception and motion. Philadelphia: W. B. Saunders & Co., 1962.
54. Weikart PS. Teaching movement and dance, a sequential approach to rhythmic movement. Ypsilanti, Mich.: The High Scope Press, 1982.
55. Harmon BD. The coordinated classroom. American Seating Company Monograph (House Springs, Mo., Circle Group International, reprinted 1983.
56. Getman GN. How to develop your child's intelligence, 3rd edition. Luverne, Minn.: Research Publications, 1962.
57. Spache GD. Investigating the issues of reading disabilities. Boston: Allyn & Bacon, 1976.
58. Penfield W, Roberts L. Speech and brain mechanisms. Princeton, NJ: Princeton University Press, 1959.
59. Kepes G. Language of vision. Chicago: Theobold & Cuneo Press, 1947.
60. Arnheim R. Visual thinking. London: Faber & Faber, 1969.
61. English HB. The historical roots of learning theory. Doubleday papers in psychology. New York: Random House, 1954.
62. Hebb DO. The organization of behavior. New York: Wiley, 1949.
63. Sherrington C. Man on his nature. Cambridge: Cambridge University Press, 1951.

64. Thurston LL. A factorial study of perception. Chicago, Ill.: Chicago University Press, 1944.
65. Armbruster F. Our children's crippled future. New York: Quadrangle (New York Times), 1977.
66. Getman GN. Are we creating more learning problems than we are curing? Learning disabilities institute, Vol. 11, Am Optom Assoc, 1982.
67. Getman GN. Computers in the classroom: bane or boon? Acad Therapy, May 1983.
68. Jackson PW. The teacher and the machine. Horace Mann Lecture, 1967. Pittsburgh: University of Pittsburgh Press, 1968.
69. Getman GN. Concepts of vision in relation to perception. Proceedings of a conference: Learning disabilities: the decade ahead. Ann Arbor, Mich.: University of Michigan, Community Services Division, 1974.
70. Getman GN. Vision, its role and integrations in learning processes. J Learning disabilities, Dec. 1981.
71. Cole L. Handwriting for left-handed children. Public School Publishing Co., 1955.
72. Springer SP, Deutsch G. Left brain, right brain. San Francisco: W. H. Freeman & Co., 1981.
73. Wunderlich R. Kids, brains and learning. St. Petersburg, Fla: Johnny Reads, Inc., 1970.
74. Getman GN. Searching for solutions or perpetuating the problems? Acad Therapy, Nov. 1977.
75. Robinson HM. Clinical studies in reading II. Supplemental Educational Monographs, No. 77. Chicago University Press, 1953.
76. Getman GN. About handwriting. Acad Therapy, Nov. 1983.
77. Betts EA. Spelling and phonics. Spelling, basic skills for effective communication. Columbus, Ohio: The Zaner-Bloser Co., 1982.
78. Hillerich RL. Let's teach spelling--not phonetic misspelling. Spelling, basic skills for effective communication. Columbus, Ohio: Zaner-Bloser, Inc., 1982.
79. Mazurkiewicz AJ. What do teachers know about phonics. Spelling, Basic skills for effective communication. Columbus, Ohio: Zaner-Bloser, Inc., 1982.
80. Benton AL. Reading disability. In J Money (Ed.) Baltimore: The Johns Hopkins Press, 1962: Chapter 6.
81. Getman GN. Where is reading readiness. Claremont Reading Conference Yearbook, 1976.
82. Levine M, Brooks R, Shonkoff J. A pediatric approach to learning disorders. New York: John Wiley & Sons, 1980.
83. Monroe M, Bracken B. Children who cannot read. Chicago: University of Chicago Press, 1944.
84. Witty P. Reading in modern education. New York: D. C. Heath & Co., 1949.

Other books available from the Optometric Extension Program:

☐ Smart in Everything...Except School $18.00
   by G.N. Getman, O.D.

☐ Suddenly Successful Student 9.00
   by Hazel Dawkins, Ellis Edelman, O.D., and
      Constantine Forkiotis, O.D.

☐ Vision and School Success 10.00
   by Lois Bing, O.D., Lillian Hinds, Ph.D., and
      George Spache, O.D.

☐ When Your Child Struggles 15.00
   by David L. Cook, O.D.

☐ Your Child's Vision 12.95
   by Richard S. Kavner, O.D.
  (Prices effective 1/95--subject to change)

☐ Please send me a free catalog

Calif. Sales Tax 7.75% / Shipping and Handling 10% (Maximum $50)

To order:
Name _____

Address _____

_____

Check enclosed __

MasterCard __ Visa __ AmX __

Card # _____

Exp. _____

OEP Foundation
2912 South Daimler Street
Santa Ana, CA 92705
Tel. (714) 250-8070 or FAX (714) 250-8157